Clear Lake Public Library
200 N. 4th Street
Clear Lake, IA 50428

THE LOYALIST

The Li ~~~~~~~~ *hnson*

B   Smith, Jeffrey K.
JOHNSON The loyalist

14

20.00

Clear Lake Public Library
200 N. 4th Street
Clear Lake, IA 50428

Copyright © 2012 Jeffrey K. Smith
All rights reserved.
ISBN-10: 1469952734
EAN-13: 9781469952734
Library of Congress Control Number: 2012901529
CreateSpace, North Charleston, SC

NOTE TO READERS

More than once, I have been questioned about the absence of footnotes or endnotes in my non-fiction books. Simply answered—it is a matter of style. While recounting the lives and times of historical figures, I have chosen to present their stories in a narrative format. It is my goal to *bring history alive,* akin to a fast-paced novel. The chronology and accuracy of the events in this book and my other works of non-fiction are substantiated by extensive research, with the sources documented in the bibliography. Ultimately, I hope the readers will understand that fact is often stranger and more compelling than fiction.

As a point of reference, a time line to Andrew Johnson's life is found at conclusion of this book.

PROLOGUE

On Good Friday, April 14, 1865, just five days after the end of the Civil War, President Abraham Lincoln was assassinated by a bitter Confederate sympathizer named John Wilkes Booth. Already torn asunder by four years of bloody war, the country struggled to come to terms with the murder of the man who had guided them through the tumultuous conflict. Lincoln became an instant martyr, and would be forever remembered as the *Great Emancipator*—a heroic, near mythical figure, who ended slavery and ultimately sacrificed his life to preserve the Union.

After Lincoln was assassinated, the commonest of men tried to fill the gigantic void. Andrew Johnson, a self-educated tailor from Tennessee, became the 17th President of the United States, and the first to enter the office after the murder of his predecessor.

Rising above an impoverished childhood, Johnson was truly a self-made man, learning a useful trade and developing his own successful business. At the same time, he rapidly ascended the political ladder—Alderman, Mayor, State Legislator, Congressman, Governor of Tennessee, United States Senator, Military Governor, Vice-President, and President of the United States.

As the only lawmaker from the South to remain in Congress after the outbreak of the Civil War, Andrew Johnson was the ultimate *Loyalist*. The Tennessee Senator was ultimately rewarded for his dedication to the Union, when he was nominated as Abraham Lincoln's running mate in the 1864 presidential election.

Unfortunately, Johnson assumed the vice-presidency under a cloud of controversy, after he delivered a drunken, disjointed inaugural address. Many Washington insiders were appalled, fearing that the new Vice-President was an alcoholic or a lunatic.

Barely a month into his vice-presidency, Johnson was thrust onto the center stage of American politics, when President Lincoln was killed, placing the Tennessean in the unenviable position of succeeding a legend. At first, the nation embraced Johnson as a worthy successor to the Great Emancipator, but the new President's obstinacy and rigid interpretation of constitutional powers ultimately led to vilification by both the Republican congressional leadership and the national press. As a result of this ill-timed political feud, Johnson's historical legacy was irrevocably damaged.

Lacking humility and burdened with a humorless personality, Johnson found it difficult to rehabilitate his tarnished reputation. When confronted by criticism, he angrily attacked his foes and assumed the role of martyr, once likening himself to Christ on the Crucifix.

In 1868, Johnson suffered the indignity of becoming the first President in American history to be impeached by the House of Representatives. By only a single vote, he avoided conviction by the Senate and forfeiture of office. Narrowly surviving this constitutional crisis, Johnson's hopes for an elected term as President were dashed.

In January of 1869, Johnson returned to Tennessee to live as a private citizen. In remarkable fashion, he managed to win election to the United States Senate, marking the first and only time that a former President has returned to serve in that legislative body.

The Loyalist: The Life and Times of Andrew Johnson is a concise biography of the 17th President of the United States, focusing upon the tumultuous years surrounding the American Civil War. Johnson was a man sustained by courage and ambition, and doomed by petulance, leading to a remarkable rise, dramatic fall, and partial vindication.

Chapter 1

They shall suffer for this

At half past ten, on Friday night, April 14, 1865, the Vice-President of the United States was sound asleep in his hotel room at the Kirkwood House in Washington D.C. During his many years of public service, Andrew Johnson had never purchased a home in the nation's Capitol. The Kirkwood House, located at the corner of Pennsylvania Avenue and 12th Street, four blocks from the White House, served as the Vice-President's formal residence. The fifty-six year-old Johnson was living alone in room number sixty-eight, while his wife and children remained in Tennessee.

The Tennessean had been sworn into office six weeks earlier, but could muster little enthusiasm for his new job. As Vice-President, Johnson's power, prestige, and overall spirits were near rock bottom. Earlier in the day, he had visited with President Lincoln at the White House—the first face-to-face meeting between the two men, since Johnson's drunken debacle on Inauguration Day. While Lincoln greeted him warmly, shaking his hand and calling him *Andy*, many Washington D.C. power brokers viewed the new Vice-President as nothing more than a semi-literate alcoholic.

It should have been a grand time for *The Loyalist*. Eleven days earlier, Richmond had fallen, and the Confederate President, Jefferson Davis, and his Cabinet were on the run, desperately attempting to elude capture by the Union Army. On April 9, 1865, Robert E. Lee had surrendered his Army of Northern Virginia to General Ulysses S. Grant, effectively ending the American Civil War. The Union had been preserved, and Abraham Lincoln was the proclaimed savior of the country. Amidst the celebration, however, Andrew Johnson was largely a forgotten figure.

On the evening of Good Friday, the Vice-President was awakened by loud knocking on the door, accompanied by a familiar, but frantic voice. Johnson's long-time friend, Leonard J. Farwell, an employee of the U.S. Patent Office and former Governor of Wisconsin, had run to the Vice-President's hotel from nearby Ford's Theater. When Johnson did not immediately answer the door, Farwell feared the worse.

"Governor Johnson, if you are in this room, I must see you!" Farwell shouted.

Half awake, the Vice-President turned up the gas light adjacent to his bed and stumbled to the door, "Farwell, is that you?"

"Yes, let me in," he answered, with a sigh of relief.

"Farwell, what on earth?" Johnson exclaimed, as he opened the unlocked door.

"I've just come from the theater. The President was shot, not ten minutes ago," Farwell breathlessly announced.

"Is he still alive?" Johnson anxiously inquired.

Having raced from Ford's Theater to the Kirkwood House immediately after the shooting, Farwell knew little about President Lincoln's condition, and was unable to provide the Vice-President with specifics.

"Go back and find out the facts," Johnson instructed him.

Farwell hurried back to the scene of the crime, only two blocks away, while the Vice-President quickly dressed. In the blink of an eye, Andrew Johnson's dull existence was no more.

At 8:30 p.m., President Lincoln and his wife, Mary Todd, along with their guests, Major Henry Rathbone and his fiancée, Clara Harris (daughter of New York Senator, Ira Harris), entered Ford's Theater to view a performance of *Our American Cousin*. The Lincoln's twelve-year-old son, Tad, was attending a performance of *Aladdin* at Grover's Theater on nearby Pennsylvania Avenue. Tad's older brother,

Robert, a twenty-two year-old Harvard graduate and Civil War veteran, was at the White House, enjoying a quiet evening of reading.

To avoid commotion, the presidential party arrived 45 minutes after opening curtain. Actress Laura Keene saw Lincoln entering his balcony level box, and suddenly ad-libbed a line, announcing the President's arrival. The performance was halted, and the orchestra, directed by William Withers, saluted the guest of honor with *Hail to the Chief*. Ever gracious, Lincoln smiled and bowed twice to the crowd of 1,500, before taking his seat in an upholstered, black walnut rocking chair. To the President's right, the First Lady settled into a high-backed chair, while Rathbone and Harris occupied a settee.

Ford's Theater had originally served as home to the First Baptist Church of Washington. When the church moved in 1861, the Ford family purchased the building and converted it into a theater. After being destroyed by fire in 1862, Ford's reopened in August of 1863. The theater boasted a seating capacity of 1,700, and was a favorite destination of Washington D.C. notables. The management was particularly honored to host the President of the United States, whose presence boosted ticket sales during what had been a slow week of business.

President Lincoln was a theater aficionado, finding stage performances a source of amusement and relaxation. With the recent surrender of the Confederate Army, ending four years of bloody war, Lincoln was ready to unwind, and an evening at Ford's Theater seemed like the perfect antidote.

While beloved by most Northerners, Abraham Lincoln was vilified by many Southerners. For one man, John Wilkes Booth, the anger festered like an open wound, and he was determined to exact revenge on behalf of the vanquished Confederacy. One of eight children, the twenty-six year-old Booth was a gifted actor, who descended from a renowned family of Thespians (his father Junius was nationally known). Ironically, John's older brother, Edwin, once saved the life of President Lincoln's oldest son, Robert, who had been inadvertently shoved from a crowded depot platform into the path of an oncoming train; Edwin alertly grabbed the younger Lincoln's coat collar and pulled him to safety.

Named for the British revolutionary, John Wilkes, the young actor was a native Marylander and rabid Confederate sympathizer. Fulfilling a promise made to his mother, he had never joined the Rebel Army, but his devotion to the Southern cause was unwavering. Booth had been enraged when President Lincoln placed his home state under martial law and imprisoned a number of Maryland Secessionists. A boastful, chronic liar, Booth was also a diehard racist, believing the black race was innately inferior.

Throughout the course of the Civil War, Booth traveled about the country, performing in various cities. The five-feet, eight-inch-tall actor was lean and muscular, with jet black hair and a stylish mustache. His striking good looks caught the eye of men and women alike. Until recently, Booth had been engaged to Lucy Lambert Hale, the daughter of Senator John Parker Hale of New Hampshire. A fellow actor described Booth in mythological terms: "Picture to yourself, Adonis."

Booth was well known to the staff and patrons of Ford's Theater. Just three weeks earlier, he had appeared on stage in *The Apostate*. In December of 1863, at Ford's Theater, President Lincoln had watched the charismatic young actor perform in *The Marble Heart*.

As the Civil War progressed and Northern victory seemed certain, Booth was no longer content with staying out of the conflict, and sought ways to revive the sinking Confederacy. The young actor had attended Lincoln's second inauguration on March 4, 1865, later bragging to a friend: "What an excellent chance I had, if I wished to kill the President on Inauguration Day! I was on the stand, and as close to him, nearly as I am to you."

With Union victory in sight, Booth's obsession with Abraham Lincoln intensified. On March 17, 1865, Booth and a small band of co-conspirators had laid in wait along the road to the *Old Soldier's Home*, three miles from Washington D.C. (the President often spent the night at this unofficial second residence, to escape the hustle and bustle of the White House). Booth had planned to kidnap Lincoln and ransom him for Confederate prisoners of war. While a change in the President's itinerary frustrated the band of would-be kidnappers on that particular evening, Booth continued to stalk Lincoln.

Three days before Lincoln's visit to Ford's Theater, Booth was among the 1,000 citizens gathered on the grounds of the White House to listen to an address by the President. Standing in an open second floor window, Lincoln read from a prepared text, outlining his post-war plans for the state of Louisiana, whereby certain freed black males would be granted the right to vote. The President's cautious remarks were aimed at those who feared the ramifications of universal black suffrage: "It is also unsatisfactory that the elective (right to vote) is not given to the colored man. I would, myself, prefer that it were now conferred on the very intelligent and on those who serve our cause as soldiers."

John Wilkes Booth was infuriated at the prospect of even limited black suffrage, explaining to his companion, David Herold: "That means Nigger citizenship. Now, by God, I'll put him through. That is the last speech he will ever give." Soon after Lincoln's speech, Booth wrote in his diary: "Something decisive must be done."

At midday, on Good Friday, Booth arrived at Ford's Theater to check his mail, and learned that both President Lincoln and General Ulysses S. Grant would be attending the evening performance; ninety minutes earlier, a White House messenger had arrived at the theater to reserve the box seats. The troubled actor realized the time was at hand for him to extract the Confederacy's revenge.

Booth quickly hatched a grandiose, but deadly plan—the assassinations of President Lincoln, Vice-President Andrew Johnson, General Grant, and Secretary of State William Seward, all on the same night. The actor believed such bold acts would leave the federal government in chaos, allowing the fragmented armies of the Confederacy to regroup and wage further war.

Booth recruited three major co-conspirators to commit the crimes of the century—Lewis Payne (also known as Lewis Powell), George Atzerodt, and David Herold. Payne (with assistance from Herold) was assigned the task of murdering Seward at his home, while Atzerodt was to kill the Vice-President in his room at the Kirk-wood House.

During the remainder of that Friday, Booth set his plan into motion. Sometime in the mid-afternoon, the actor entered the lobby of the Kirkwood House and handed the desk clerk a letter addressed to Vice-President Johnson: "Don't wish to disturb you. Are you at home? J. Wilkes Booth." The motivation for this rather bizarre action remains unknown, but many believe Booth was try-ing to confirm the Vice-President's schedule for the remainder of the afternoon and evening, so that Atzerodt could more easily carry out his murderous assignment. Johnson, however, never answered the actor's written inquiry.

Later in the day, when the actor returned to his room at the Na-tional Hotel, on the corner of Pennsylvania Avenue and 6th Street, where he had been staying for the past several days, Booth asked a clerk if he planned to attend Ford's Theater that night.

"There is going to be some splendid acting tonight," the actor boldly predicted.

That afternoon, as he traveled the city streets on horseback, Booth encountered General Grant and his wife, Julia, who were traveling to the train station. Grant had politely declined the Pres-ident's invitation to attend the theater, opting instead to visit his children in New Jersey (Mrs. Grant, in particular, detested Mary Todd Lincoln). Booth rode past Grant's luggage-filled carriage twice, glar-ing at the famed general.

"I thought he was going to Ford's tonight," Booth remarked to a bystander.

"Somebody said he's going to New Jersey," the man replied.

Unknowingly, General Grant had removed himself from Booth's macabre fantasy.

When Booth happened to run into John Matthews, he gave his fellow actor a sealed letter. He asked Matthews to make sure the letter was published in the *National Intelligencer* newspaper, in the event Booth had to leave town "suddenly." Matthews placed the envelope in his coat pocket, unaware of its shocking contents: "For a long time, I have devoted my energies, my time and money, to the accomplishment of a certain end. I have been disappointed. The moment has arrived when I must change my plans. Many will blame me for what I am about to do, but posterity, I am sure, will justify me; men who love their country better than gold and life." The letter was signed: "John W. Booth, Payne, Herold, and Atzerodt." The narcissistic actor was determined the world would know who was responsible for the history making events about to unfold.

In preparation for the presidential visit, workers at Ford's Theater had removed the pinewood partition between Boxes Seven and Eight on the second floor upper level, creating a larger private viewing area for Lincoln and his guests. The box's twin balustrades were draped with the Stars and Stripes, and a blue United States Treasury Guards flag was hung from the center pillar. A framed engraving of George Washington sat just below the regimental flag, looking out over the crowd.

Preparing for his command performance, John Wilkes Booth had dinner at the National Hotel. Shortly after 9:00 p.m., the flamboyant actor, dressed in a black frock coat, black pants, thigh high riding boots with spurs, and a black hat, rode his horse into Baptist Alley, at the rear of Ford's Theater. Booth recruited a Ford's employee, Edward Spangler, to hold his horse, while he took care of business inside the building. Spangler soon had to shift stage scenery, and asked fellow handyman, Joseph "Peanuts" Burroughs, to tend the actor's steed.

Booth, who knew the layout of Ford's Theater like the back of his hand, entered the backstage door while the play was in progress. Using a passageway below the stage and a little known hallway, Booth was able to reach the theater lobby without his route of entry being noticed. Exiting the building onto 10th Street, he walked next door to Taltavull's Saloon. After fortifying his courage with several shots of whiskey, the actor reentered the theater through the front door and nonchalantly chatted with ticket collector, John Buckingham.

The presence of the famous actor at Ford's was a routine occurrence, and no one took particular notice when he ascended the winding staircase to the second floor. At the dress circle level, Booth encountered two Union Army officers, who recognized him, but soon turned their attention back to the stage. Approaching the vestibule, just outside the presidential box, Booth was delighted to discover that his prey was essentially unprotected.

Washington police officer, John F. Parker, who was Lincoln's assigned body guard, had a well-deserved reputation as a lazy, uneducated drunkard. The thirty-four year-old Virginian had served in the Union Army for three months, before joining the D.C. Metropolitan Police Department in 1861. Parker had previously been disciplined for drunk and disorderly behavior, after he swore at citizens and a supervising police officer.

After President Lincoln and his party settled into their seats, Parker exited the theater to have a drink at the next door saloon Booth had just vacated. This inexcusable lapse in security occurred at a time when Lincoln had more than eighty written death threats tucked in the cubbyhole of his presidential desk.

The only man between John Wilkes Booth and his infamous place in history was presidential valet, Charles Forbes, who sat adjacent to the unlocked box door. After studying Booth's calling card, Forbes mistakenly assumed the President wanted to meet with the famous actor, and allowed him to pass.

Inside the vestibule, Booth found a pine rod (a piece of a music stand), which he had hidden inside the darkened room earlier in the day. After he wedged the piece of wood between the door and the adjacent wall, routine entry into the presidential box would be impossible. Booth then gazed through the peephole that he had earlier bored into the door leading to the balcony. Inside the box, the President, First Lady, and their guests were intently focused on the stage below.

Booth silently opened the inner door and lurked in the shadows of the box, observing the President, who was leaning slightly forward in the rocking chair, holding his wife's hand. Quietly, the actor reached into the pockets of his frock coat and removed a .44 caliber, single shot, brass-barreled, muzzle loaded derringer, and a 7-inch, razor-sharp dagger (commonly known as a Rio Grande

Camp Knife). The actor carefully aimed the tiny pistol at the back of Abraham Lincoln's head.

At 10:13 p.m., during Act Three, Scene Two of *Our American Cousin*, the crack of a single gunshot echoed throughout Ford's Theater. President Lincoln slumped forward, as smoke from the gunpowder wafted out of the box. After a few seconds of stunned silence, Major Rathbone realized that Booth had fired the shot, and tried to subdue the attacker. Athletic and a masterful swordsman, Booth eluded Rathbone's charge and quickly disabled the military officer with a vicious stab to the arm. Bleeding and in great pain, Rathbone slumped to the floor.

Actor, Harry Hawk, performing on the stage below, was distracted by the commotion in the presidential box: "My God, that's John Booth!"

Ever the actor, Booth crawled over the balcony railing and leapt to the stage, eleven feet below. The spurs on Booth's right boot snagged the fabric of the regimental flag, causing him to land unevenly on the floor, fracturing his left fibula, two inches above the ankle. In spite of the pain, Booth finished his performance with an oratorical flourish: "Sic Temper Tyrannis" ("Thus always to tyrants"—the Virginia state motto).

The theater patrons were temporarily confused, wondering if Booth's performance was a macabre, unscripted revision of the play. For several seconds, no one seemed to know what to do.

"The South is avenged!" Booth shouted, before limping across the stage.

William Withers stepped in front of Booth, who slashed him, cutting the orchestra director's coat and vest, and inflicting a superficial wound. At the back stage door, Jake Ritterspaugh, the set carpenter, attempted to block Booth's escape. The murderous actor slashed at Ritterspaugh, who was forced to back away. Exiting the rear of the theater, Booth mounted his horse, kicking Joseph Burroughs to the ground.

"He kicked me! He kicked me!" Burroughs screamed.

In a clutter of hoof beats, the assassin fled the scene of the crime.

Delighted by his triumph, Booth was also in severe pain from his broken leg. Within minutes of escaping Ford's Theater, the actor approached the Navy Yard Bridge that spanned the Potomac River. Booth hoped to cross the river and find safe haven among Confederate sympathizers, first in Maryland, then Virginia.

The Union Army sentry guarding the bridge, Silas T. Cobb, halted the anxious horseman: "Who are you, sir?"

"My name is Booth," the actor answered.

"Where are you going?" the sentry asked.

"I'm going home," Booth lied.

When Cobb asked Booth where he lived, the actor lied effortlessly: "I live close to Beantown, but do not live in the town."

Cobb inquired why Booth was out so late, explaining that no one was routinely allowed to cross the bridge after 9:00 p.m. John Wilkes Booth, acting out the role of a lifetime, explained that he was unaware of the curfew, and hoped to travel home by the light of the moon. The murderous actor's performance proved convincing, and Cobb allowed Booth to cross the bridge and escape into the vast countryside.

In his hotel room, Andrew Johnson anxiously awaited an update from Leonard Farwell. Up to this point, Johnson's evening had been routine; the Vice-President and Farwell had shared an early dinner at the Kirkwood House, before parting company. While Farwell headed to Ford's theater, Johnson had prepared for bed. Now, with a single gunshot, Good Friday turned into the longest night of Johnson's life.

The Vice-President was still unaware of his own good luck. Earlier in the day, John Wilkes Booth had met with co-conspirator, George Atzerodt, providing the young man with a revolver and knife: "You must kill Johnson."

Atzerodt, a twenty-nine year-old Prussian immigrant, was a devoted secessionist. He owned a carriage repair business in Port Tobacco, Maryland, and also smuggled contraband across the Potomac River into Virginia. Atzerodt's extensive knowledge of the roads connecting Washington D.C. to the Deep South was a major asset to Booth's master plan.

Preparing to assassinate the Vice-President, Atzerodt rented a room, one floor above Johnson's Kirkwood House suite. Authorities later discovered a revolver, Bowie knife, and bank deposit book (bearing the name of John Wilkes Booth) in Atzerodt's hotel room.

In many respects, Atzerodt's assigned task was easier than Booth's—the Vice-President was essentially alone, in an unguarded and unlocked room. Booth instructed Atzerodt to knock on Johnson's door, shoot the Vice-President, and immediately flee the scene of the crime. Afterwards, Atzerodt was supposed to rendezvous with the other assassins in the Maryland countryside. As the night progressed, however, the would-be assassin medicated his growing anxiety with alcohol, and grew less certain about the prospect of committing murder. Eventually, Atzerodt lost his nerve and exited the hotel, leaving Johnson unharmed.

Secretary of State, William Seward, did not share the Vice-President's good fortune. The sixty-four year-old Seward was recuperating from serious orthopedic and internal injuries suffered in a carriage accident a week earlier. Bedridden inside his three-story brick house at Lafayette Park, within site of the White House, Seward and his family were accosted by another Booth co-conspirator, Lewis Payne.

Only twenty-one years-old, Payne was a muscular six-footer, with a deformed face—the result of having been kicked by a mule. A seasoned veteran of the Confederate Army and former agent of the Confederate Secret Service, Payne was an ardent Rebel sympathizer. After being wounded and captured at Gettysburg, he returned to the Washington D.C. area.

When Payne and Herold arrived outside Seward's house, the latter minded the horses and mentally formulated an escape route. A pharmacy clerk, the twenty-two year-old Herold was accustomed to making medication deliveries, and was well-acquainted with the capitol city's streets and alleyways.

Pretending to be a messenger delivering medication from Seward's physician, Payne forced his way inside the Secretary of

State's home and proceeded upstairs. Encountering resistance from Seward's son, Frederick, Payne tried to shoot him, but his revolver misfired. Using the pistol as a club, Payne fractured Frederick's skull, exposing raw brain tissue. The impact from the blows to the younger Seward's head completely disabled the weapon's firing mechanism, rendering it useless.

Forcing his way past Seward's daughter and stabbing the soldier assigned to guard the Secretary of State, Payne turned his knife on his intended target. Seward's bed was pushed against wall, literally hemming him in, as Payne made repeated, wicked lashes with the sharp blade, staining the bedcovers with blood.

"Murder!" Seward's daughter screamed out the open second-floor window.

After hearing Miss Seward's panicked screams, a frightened David Herold fled the scene, hoping to link up with the master planner, John Wilkes Booth, in the Maryland countryside.

Fighting through the pain of his stab wounds, Seward's military guard attempted to tackle Payne. The two men struggled for a moment, before Payne fled the house, muttering: "I'm mad."

Amazingly, Seward recovered from the knife wounds. Even though he sustained severe lacerations to the neck and face, causing permanent facial paralysis, no major blood vessels were severed, and the Secretary of State would eventually return to his Cabinet position.

Meanwhile, Andrew Johnson paced the floor of his hotel suite, awaiting word on President Lincoln's fate. Eventually, Leonard Farwell returned and reported that the President was still alive, but critically wounded, and had been transported to a private home across the street from Ford's Theater. Johnson immediately reached for his hat and coat.

"You can't go out of the hotel," Farwell pleaded.

"My friend is in trouble," Johnson replied, "I must go to him."

By now, the Kirkwood House was under armed guard, and the Provost Marshal of the District of Columbia, James R. O'Beirne, summoned troops to accompany the Vice-President on his excursion to

Lincoln's bedside. Johnson, unaccustomed to depending on others for his personal safety, declined the offer, and departed on foot, accompanied by Farwell and O'Beirne, only.

The bullet fired by John Wilkes Booth struck Abraham Lincoln in the back of the head, near his left ear. The .44 caliber ball shattered Lincoln's skull and penetrated deeply into his brain, lodging behind the President's right eye. The gun shot rendered Lincoln immediately unconscious.

Blood streaming from his arm, Major Rathbone managed to remove the pine bar wedged against the door, allowing theater patron, Doctor Charles Augustus Leale, to attend to the fallen President. A twenty-three year-old graduate of Bellevue Hospital Medical College, Leale was working at the U. S. Army General Hospital in Washington D. C., and had come to the theater dressed in his military uniform.

Eyes closed, with his head nodding forward, the President was held upright by the First Lady, who exclaimed: "Oh, Doctor! Is he dead? Can he recover?"

After lowering him to the floor, Leale located the bullet wound in the back of Lincoln's head. Using his little finger, the physician removed a clot and decreased the growing pressure on the President's brain. After performing artificial respiration on the patient, Leale was able to detect a feeble pulse. The physician, however, offered little hope: "His wound is mortal—it is impossible for him to recover."

With no stretcher available, four soldiers carried an unconscious Lincoln down the stairs to the lobby, where he was placed atop the pine partition that had been removed to create the presidential box. The mortally wounded President was carried on the makeshift stretcher out of the theater and into the street, where confusion reigned.

Lincoln's carriage was available to transport the President to the White House, but the physicians overruled this plan, fearing the bouncing ride would cause the bullet to inflict further brain damage. Someone in the crowd suggested taking Lincoln into Taltavull's

Saloon, but that location was deemed undignified. Just then, Henry Safford, a boarder at the three-story home of William Petersen at 453 10th Street, just across from the theater, stepped out on the first floor porch.

Eyeing the confusion, Safford called out: "Bring him here! Bring him here!"

Lincoln was carried into the house and settled into a rear bedroom, rented by Private William T. Clark of the 13th Massachusetts Infantry. Placed diagonally on a bed too short for his six-feet, four-inch frame, Lincoln was evaluated by other physicians (including Joseph Burns, the Surgeon General of the Army, and Charles Crone, the future Surgeon General), all of whom concurred with Leale's prognosis—survival was impossible.

Secretary of War, Edwin Stanton, having learned of the attacks against President Lincoln and Secretary of State Seward, rushed to the Petersen residence, accompanied by the Secretary of Navy, Gideon Welles. The bespectacled, fifty-one year-old Stanton with his bushy, chest length, graying beard and unsmiling countenance, was considered Lincoln's most trusted advisor.

Stanton was stunned to see his Commander-in-Chief in dire straits, and immediately reflected on the unfairness of the situation, so soon after the long-awaited and triumphant conclusion of the Civil War. The Secretary of War remembered visiting Lincoln earlier in the day at the White House: "He was more cheerful than I had ever seen him."

Stanton quickly transformed his grief into action, taking charge of the tragic and chaotic situation. The Secretary of War stationed himself at Lincoln's bedside, while occasionally moving to a makeshift Cabinet room in the parlor across the hall. Stanton telegraphed military leaders around the country, notifying them of the assassination attempts against the President and Secretary of State. The first wire, dispatched at 1:30 a.m., described Lincoln's wound as "mortal," and reported the President was "now dying." When eyewitnesses at Ford's Theater identified John Wilkes Booth as the shooter, Stanton telegraphed this information to his field commanders. The

Secretary of War also assigned military guards for the Vice-President and other Cabinet officers.

Mary Todd Lincoln, histrionic by nature, was overwhelmed by the grave injury to her husband, and wailed loudly, over and over, at his bedside. Blunt and abrasive, Stanton was angered and unnerved by the First Lady's outbursts, and brusquely ordered her out of the room.

At 2:00 a.m., Vice-President Johnson arrived at the Petersen House, and confirmed his worst fears; Lincoln's prognosis was grim. Johnson did not interfere with Secretary Stanton's supervisory role, and remained at the President's bedside for only thirty minutes. Aware that Mrs. Lincoln detested him, the Vice-President felt like an unwanted intruder, and returned to his room at the Kirkwood House.

A light rain fell through the long night, as Johnson received periodic updates concerning Lincoln's rapidly deteriorating condition. Pacing the floor, he maintained a death vigil. When the Vice-President learned of John Wilkes Booth's pro-Confederate sympathies, he impulsively condemned the radical element in the South: "They shall suffer for this. They shall suffer for this."

Chapter 2

Mudsill

The 17th President of the United States was born in a log cabin in Raleigh, North Carolina on December 29, 1808. Andrew Johnson's city of birth, while designated as the state capitol, was little more than a small town, with roughly 1,000 occupants, a third of whom were African Americans.

An apocryphal tale has long claimed that Johnson was named for General Andrew Jackson. However, there is scant evidence to support this story, and it is more likely that Andrew was named after an uncle. Regardless of the genesis of the name, he was simply called Andrew Johnson—no middle name or initial.

Andrew was one of three children born to Jacob and Mary Mc-Donough Johnson. His older brother, William, was born in 1804, while a sister, Elizabeth, died in childhood. Jacob Johnson was among the poorest of the white citizens in Raleigh, and never achieved the status of property owner. Hardworking, but illiterate, Jacob was employed in a variety of positions—miller, porter at the State Bank of North Carolina, constable, janitor at the state Capitol Building, hostler, and city bell ringer.

Andrew's mother, Mary, was a gifted seamstress, and many town folk referred to her as *Polly the Weaver*. Like her husband, Mary toiled to help the family eek out a meager existence, with little hope of socioeconomic advancement. For a time, both of Andrew's parents were employed by Casso's Inn; Mary worked as a weaver, and Jacob as a hostler. At one point, Mary worked as a seamstress and laundress for John Haywood, a noted attorney in Raleigh. Young

Andrew bore a strong resemblance to Haywood, giving rise to unfounded rumors that he was the lawyer's illegitimate son.

Tragedy struck the Johnson family when Andrew was three years old. Jacob rescued three people from drowning in Hunter Mill's Pond, after their small boat had capsized. Thomas Henderson, the renowned publisher of the *Raleigh Star* newspaper, was among those saved. The elder Johnson was immediately hailed as a hero, but his notoriety was short-lived. While ringing the town bell in celebration of the rescue, Jacob collapsed and died, presumably from a stroke or heart attack. Dirt poor, Jacob Johnson was buried in an unmarked grave in the potter's field.

Now penniless and fatherless, Andrew Johnson's future was bleak. The Johnson family dwelled on the second lowest social tier in the community—they were called *mudsills*—synonymous with *white trash*. Only the Negroes in the Raleigh area were considered inferior to the mudsills.

Throughout his life, Andrew would never completely outgrow his mudsill roots. A burning desire for personal success and an unwavering prejudice about the inferiority of the black race were lasting by-products of Johnson's early social and economic impoverishment.

Johnson's opportunities for advancement seemed remote. At the time, Raleigh had no public school system, and private schooling was cost prohibitive for the poor. When Mary Johnson remarried, three years after Jacob's death, the economic outlook for the family remained dim. Andrew's stepfather, Turner Daughtry, was as poor and illiterate as his biological father.

To help support his impoverished family, Andrew was forced to learn a useful trade. His older brother, William, was already serving as a tailor's apprentice. At age ten, Andrew was apprenticed to J. Selby's Tailor Shop with a binding contract: "Ordered that A. Johnson, an orphan boy and the son of Jacob Johnson, deceased, be bound to Jas. J. Selby till he arrive at the lawful age (twenty-one) to learn the trade of tailor."

While sitting cross-legged on the floor cutting cloth patterns and stitching them into jackets, vests, and trousers, Andrew Johnson dreamed of much greater things. He yearned for the education his family could not afford. His hopes were answered, in part, when a handful of Raleigh's more learned citizens visited the tailor's shop and read to the apprentices. While many of the apprentices were indifferent to the prospects of literacy, Johnson reveled in the opportunity to combine work with education. Assisted by Dr. William Hill, one of the tailor shop's regular customers, Andrew learned to read, and developed a lifelong passion for books. Determined to rise above his mudsill roots, he often spent two to three hours per night, reading and studying.

The American Speaker, a collection of inspiring political orations by British and American statesmen, became one of Johnson's favorites, and he often borrowed the book from Dr. Hill. Eventually, Hill gave Andrew his own copy of *The American Speaker.* The young apprentice tailor memorized entire passages from the book, and one of his favorite lines became a fitting metaphor for his life: "The best and most meritorious public successes have always been performed by persons removed from opulence."

For the remainder of his life, Johnson remained an avid reader. His grasp of history and literature were impressive for someone without formal schooling, but the deficiencies in his self-education were manifested in his writings, which contained spelling, punctuation, and grammatical errors.

The young apprentice soaked up the political conversation and informal debates between prominent local officials. Andrew studied how different people framed their arguments, and committed their styles to memory. By the time he was an adult, Johnson would be a formidable orator.

As he read more about history and politics, Johnson came to idolize Andrew Jackson. *Old Hickory* embodied the characteristics that captured the imagination of an impoverished boy—fearlessness, compassion for the underdog, and iron resolve. Jackson would forever remain a symbolic hero to Andrew Johnson.

As young Andrew expanded his intellectual boundaries, his temper and impulsiveness were often problematic—a pattern that would repeat itself in the years to come. In June of 1924, when Johnson was not yet sixteen, he hurled a rock through the window of a house owned by an affluent Raleigh citizen. Whether motivated by class envy, as some suspected, or simply a mischievous impulse, the act of vandalism placed Andrew and his brother (who accompanied him during the misadventure) at risk for being arrested. Running away seemed like the only logical solution for the youthful mudsills.

The Johnson brothers fled Raleigh, walking some fifty miles southwest, to the town of Carthage. Andrew immediately went to work as a journeyman tailor, but knew that as along he remained in the state of North Carolina, he risked being arrested and prosecuted, not only for vandalism, but also for violation of his apprentice contract.

Johnson's fears proved well founded, when James Selby placed a newspaper ad, dated June 24, 1824, offering a $10.00 reward: "I will pay the above reward to any person who will deliver said apprentices to me in Raleigh, or I will give the above reward for Andrew Johnson, alone. All persons are cautioned against harboring or employing said apprentices on pain of being prosecuted."

With the prospects of eluding capture in North Carolina appearing grim, after a few months, Andrew and his brother headed south on foot, finally stopping in the upstate South Carolina town of Laurens. In the Palmetto State, Andrew found employment in a local tailor's shop, where his skills were greatly appreciated. During his off hours, Johnson continued his self-education, devouring as many books as he could borrow.

For a time, it appeared the young tailor had found a new home. After meeting a local girl, Mary Woods, Andrew presented her with a token of his affection—a hand-stitched quilt. Johnson soon followed with a marriage proposal, which was abruptly turned down, as the young lady's family saw limited potential in the poor, journeyman tailor. Once again, Johnson endured the humiliating sting of social and economic prejudice.

Rejected and dispirited, Andrew returned to North Carolina after a two-year stint in Laurens, where he sought out James Selby in hopes of being released from his apprenticeship. Selby insisted on a lump sum cash settlement before voiding the contract. The cost was far greater than Johnson could afford, leaving him with few options, as he was prohibited from working as a tailor in North Carolina until his twenty-first birthday. Proud, but demoralized, the mudsill would have to start anew outside of his home state.

Chapter 3

A. Johnson, Tailor

In the fall of 1825, when he was not yet seventeen years old, Andrew Johnson left North Carolina for the second time. While mature beyond his years, he was still impoverished, and owned no property, not even a horse. Utilizing the only affordable transportation available, Johnson began walking toward the west. Along the way, he managed to hitch a wagon ride, which carried him to Knoxville, Tennessee. On a flatboat, the journeyman floated down the Tennessee River to Mooresville, Alabama, finding employment in a tailor's shop. Johnson eventually moved to Columbia, Tennessee and worked for a time.

After six months, a restless Johnson returned to Raleigh. His indentured status remained unsettled, leaving him no opportunity to utilize his only marketable skill in his home state. After discussing the future with his family, all of whom were living at or near the poverty level, a decision was made to leave North Carolina for good.

Packing all their worldly belongings into a two-wheeled cart pulled by a blind horse, Andrew, along with his mother, step-father, brother, and another young tailor left Raleigh on foot. A new beginning beckoned beyond the mountains of Western Carolina.

In September of 1826, Andrew and his family reached the small town of Greeneville, Tennessee, just across the North Carolina state line. Bordered by the majestic Smoky Mountains, Greeneville was the county seat, and one of the oldest communities in Eastern Tennessee. Greene County was an antebellum anomaly, with only 1070 of its 14,140 African Americans living as slaves. The mountainous, local terrain was better suited to sustenance farming and raising livestock, as opposed to cotton plantations, and there was a reduced need for slave labor. With such a small percentage of slave owners living in the area, Greeneville's white citizens had less interest in *States' Rights* and the burgeoning *Secessionist* movement than many of their fellow Southerners.

After settling his family into rented rooms in the back of a tavern, Andrew went to work at George Boyle's Tailor Shop, determined to build a future in his adopted state. For unknown reasons, Johnson briefly moved to nearby Rutledge, Tennessee, before returning to Greeneville and opening his own tailor's shop in March of 1827. The newly established businessman proudly displayed his store front sign: *A. Johnson, Tailor.*

Johnson also fell in love, and for the first time, his affection was welcomed and returned. Eliza McCardle, whose deceased father, John, had been a shoe maker, helped her mother sew quilts. Eliza's social and financial position was no better than Andrew's, preventing class discrimination from standing in the way of romance. She was immediately smitten with Johnson, even before the two started dating, telling her mother: "There goes the man I'm going to marry." Her dreams were prescient, and the young couple was married on May 17, 1827 in Eliza's hometown of Warrensburg, Tennessee. Justice of the Peace, Mordecai Lincoln, second cousin to a young Illinois attorney named Abraham Lincoln, presided over the wedding ceremony between the eighteen year-old groom and his sixteen year-old bride.

The marriage between Andrew and Eliza lasted for the remainder of their lives, and produced five children—two daughters and three sons (Martha, Mary, Charles, Robert, and Andrew Jr.). Eliza, who suffered from tuberculosis, was often sick and frequently avoided social events, and later in life, the Johnson's daughter, Martha, filled the void by serving as her father's official hostess.

Eliza was quiet and introspective, unlike her fiery, outspoken husband. Tennessee State Senator, George Washington Jones, remembered the Johnson's enduring marriage: "Their temperaments were unlike—he, fervid and aggressive—she calm and retiring—

but, their union was fortunate, and he was better prepared for the long encounter, which fate held in reserve."

Andrew rented a house on Greeneville's Main Street, setting up his tailor shop in the front, and living quarters in the rear. Eliza, the beneficiary of a solid education, often read to her husband as he sewed, and helped him learn to write and master basic arithmetic skills, fostering his non-formal education. Johnson was particularly interested in books on politics and oratory, and soon dreamed of a future beyond sewing and stitching. Ambitious in her own right, Eliza was a sound money manager, and helped her husband invest wisely in real estate.

Johnson earned a reputation as an excellent tailor, charging $3.50 for a coat, $1.50 for a pair of trousers, $3.50 for a vest, and $10.00 for a complete suit. Johnson's account books from 1831-1842 documented his prodigious labor: 94 vests, 97 pairs of pants, 356 coats, 71 half-coats, and 7 suits. Customers who could not pay for clothing with cash, often bartered with firewood or produce. Johnson was proud of his craftsmanship: "My work never ripped or gave way."

As his business grew, Johnson took on a business partner and also employed journeymen tailors. Eventually, he was able to purchase a larger building, and moved his tailor's shop to a more prominent location, on the corner of College and Depot Streets. Later in life, Johnson summed up his successful business philosophy: "When I was a tailor, I always made a close fit and was always punctual to my customers, and did good work."

Johnson's business became a gathering place for local civic leaders, where politics was the prime topic of conversation. As Andrew's interest in public affairs continued to grow, he joined a local debating society. Committed to improving his oratorical skills, the young tailor walked four miles to Greeneville College to observe and participate in weekly debates.

Johnson remained a dedicated supporter of his fellow Tennessean, Andrew Jackson. Even though he had not yet declared himself a *Democrat*, Johnson could not abide the policies of the rival *Whig* Party. The Whigs, a legacy of the early *Federalist* Party, believed the strength of the country resided in the hands of the powerful and affluent citizenry—a notion Johnson flatly rejected. Andrew openly denounced Whiggery, championing the rights of the working man.

Only nineteen years-old, the rapidly-maturing Johnson had already married and developed a successful business. Dark complexioned, with fierce black eyes, the five-foot, eight-inch Johnson was solidly built, weighing one-hundred seventy-five pounds. With broad shoulders, squat neck, and prominent brow, his stern countenance was a perfect complement to his unyielding personality. Johnson viewed the world in black and white terms—"rich versus poor," and "right versus wrong." Once his mind was made up on an issue, there was little hope of changing it. Johnson's dogged devotion to his side of an argument often exhausted or demoralized his opponents. A fellow debater complimented the young tailor on his style: "There was no hurried utterance. He held his crowd spellbound."

Eliza soon urged her ambitious husband to showcase his oratorical skills in the public arena. Johnson needed little encouragement to leap into the world of politics.

Chapter 4

Three-fifths of a white male

Though not yet twenty, Andrew Johnson seemed older and more mature than his years. Having built a thriving business from the ground up, the young tailor caught the eye of his fellow citizens, who applauded his work ethic and leadership qualities. In 1829, the admiring townspeople elected the young tailor as Alderman. Johnson approached his duties in city government with the same energy and fiscal discipline that he applied to his business. A year later, his fellow Aldermen chose Johnson to serve as Mayor of Greeneville.

Impeccably dressed and well spoken, the new Mayor gained further recognition when he joined the 19th Regiment of the Tennessee Militia, and was awarded the rank of Colonel. As his financial standing continued to improve, Johnson was able to build a new house across the street from his tailor's shop, and purchased a nearby farm (serving as home for his mother and stepfather).

Johnson also became a slave owner, purchasing a fourteen year-old girl named Dolly and her half-brother Sam. Dolly reportedly encouraged Johnson to buy her because she thought he "looked kind." Dolly later gave birth to three children, who were registered as "mulattoes" on the census records, giving rise to rumors that Johnson was their father. Johnson indeed treated Dolly's children as if they were his own, playing with them, holding them in his lap, and buying them presents. Johnson eventually acquired over a half-dozen African Americans, all of whom worked as house servants. Later in life, Sam often boasted about being Johnson's servant. Martha Johnson, fully aware of her father's benevolence, described the relationship in different terms: "But in truth, Andrew Johnson belonged to Sam." While treating his slaves with kindness, Johnson maintained a steadfast belief in the superiority of the white race.

Johnson's involvement in politics coincided with the beginnings of a nationwide sectional debate over slavery. Slavery had established its roots in North America in 1619, when 20 captive Africans were brought to Jamestown, Virginia. Eventually, slaves were imported to all 13 colonies. By the middle of the 18th century, virtually every black person in what would become the United States of America was a slave.

During the Revolutionary War, American slave trade was temporarily ended by the First Continental Congress, as part of a boycott on external commerce. In 1784, while serving as Virginia's elected congressional representative under the Articles of Confederation (which predated the U.S. Constitution), Thomas Jefferson drafted a bill, prohibiting slavery in the Northwest Territory (an area comprising the future states of Ohio, Michigan, Wisconsin, Illinois, and Indiana). Jefferson, who hoped to prevent the extension of slavery to all new states, saw his legislative proposal defeated by one vote.

"The voice of a single individual...would have prevented this abominable crime from spreading itself over the new country," the future President lamented.

Slave importation eventually resumed in the Southern colonies (namely S. Carolina and Georgia). In 1808, the federal government decreed an end to slave importation, though illegal traders smuggled some 7000 Africans into the United States over the next 10 years.

Prior to federal prohibition of slave trade, a handful of non-agrarian Northern states (Vermont, Pennsylvania, and Massachusetts) had already abolished slavery. In Southern states, where cash crops like cotton, tobacco, rice, and indigo were the mainstays of the economy, slavery flourished. Virginian and framer of the American Constitution, James Madison, recognized the necessity of slave labor in his home state and other regions of the

South. Madison viewed slaves as property, rather than sovereign citizens, writing that African Americans had "no claim" or "attention" from Congress. At the same time, the ever-growing slave population represented a political boon for Southerners, who insisted that the Constitution designate individual slaves as *three-fifths* of a white male, for purposes of congressional representation.

As the frontier west of the Mississippi River rapidly populated, Southern Democrats and Northern Whigs took opposing positions on the expansion of slavery. Southerners vigorously opposed any limitation of involuntary servitude in the expanding territorial lands. In contrast, Northerners did not want to see the Democratic Party gain further congressional power through the admission of new slave states into the Union. The Whig Party also gained the support of a burgeoning group of *Abolitionists*, who were morally opposed to the institution of slavery.

In 1820, Congress brokered a deal acceptable to both Northern and Southern interests. The so-called *Missouri Compromise* prohibited slavery in the former Louisiana Territory north of the 36 degree, 30 minute parallel, excluding the state of Missouri. In 1820, Maine was admitted as a free state, and a year later, Missouri joined the Union as a slave state. For the next 16 years, no new states were added. In 1836, Arkansas was admitted as a slave state, followed by Michigan (as a free state), maintaining an acceptable regional balance, and forestalling conflict between the North and South.

While Andrew Johnson considered slaves to be personal property, and supported the westward expansion of slavery, he vehemently disagreed with many of his fellow Southerners on the right of *secession* as a means to defend their established way of life. Johnson's hero, Andrew Jackson, had firmly established a policy that individual states could not nullify federal law and remove themselves from the Union. Johnson embraced Jackson's *Unionist* position, and developed an unwavering belief in the sanctity of an undivided country.

In 1834, Andrew Johnson was named a trustee for Rhea Academy, a local private school. For a man who had never attended a day of formal school, the prestigious appointment was a source of pride, and further vindication of his exhaustive efforts at self-improvement.

While he was viewed as a prosperous, model citizen, Johnson's trademark temper occasionally flared. In August of 1834, a fellow Greenevillian, Thomas McLay, filed charges against Johnson for "assault and battery." The exact nature of their dispute is not known, but Johnson was fined $100.00. However, when the plaintiff failed to appear at the scheduled court date, the charges and fine were dismissed.

In 1834, the state of Tennessee drafted a new Constitution to replace the original document drawn up in 1796. While the new Constitution eliminated a number of property ownership qualifications required to vote and seek office, the disenfranchisement of free blacks was continued. Adopting the contradictory position of both *populist* and *white supremacist*, Johnson campaigned vigorously for passage of the new document.

Now fully invested in local politics, Andrew Johnson began to look beyond Greeneville. In 1835, when such an opportunity arose, the tailor from Tennessee made his move.

Chapter 5

I too, am in the fight

By 1835, Tennessee's population had grown to the extent that further legislative representation was necessary. A new state legislator, designated as a *floater*, was authorized for Greene and Washington Counties. After two prominent Greeneville citizens announced their candidacy for the state legislature, Andrew Johnson followed suit: "I, too am in the fight."

As the campaign unfolded, Johnson proved to be the most skilled debater, and one opponent quickly withdrew. On Election Day, the 27 year-old Johnson won in a landslide (by a vote of 1413 to 80).

After his election to the legislature, Johnson leased out his tailor's shop and headed for Nashville, arriving in October of 1835. Eliza, whose health was chronically poor, remained at home, while her husband shared a rented room with another representative. At the time, Nashville was not yet the permanent capitol of Tennessee, and there was no Capitol building, forcing the legislature to congregate on the third floor of the public courthouse. Perched on the banks of the Cumberland River, Nashville was home to some 6,000 residents, and was the largest city Andrew Johnson had ever seen.

Johnson had not yet declared an official party allegiance, but his populism and admiration of the Democratic President, Andrew Jackson, guided his political orientation. However, Johnson refused to follow strict party lines, voting his conscience on each issue. He soon cultivated relationships with political leaders throughout the state—a move that would prove beneficial to his political future.

A fiscal conservative, Representative Johnson discouraged *non-essential* government expenditures. He also opposed the extension of railroads, fearing drovers (wagon haulers) and inns in rural portions of the state would be bypassed, and put out of business.

Consistent with his belief in the inferiority of the black race, Johnson supported the firm oversight and control of the free black population, and considered African Americans intellectually unqualified to participate in the electoral process. At the same time, Johnson realized that some people viewed slavery as morally wrong, and refused to support a proposed *Anti-Abolitionist Bill*.

After his first legislative session, lasting nearly four months, Johnson returned to Greeneville. He was shocked to find his popularity had plummeted, as many constituents were angered by his opposition to the expansion of the railroad industry. A local physician, Brookins Campbell, eventually challenged Johnson in his bid for re-election. After a hard fought campaign, the challenger unseated the incumbent; for the first time in his political career, Johnson felt the sting of defeat.

Johnson responded to the loss by more forcefully asserting his populist agenda. After formally declaring his loyalty to the Democratic Party, Johnson regained his legislative seat in the 1839 election. Returning to Nashville, he remained a determined watchdog for the taxpayers, and refused to support any bills entailing frivolous spending.

Johnson gradually built a loyal and powerful political machine in East Tennessee. The Democratic State Convention rewarded Johnson's growing influence by choosing him as one of two state electors in the 1840 presidential election. Johnson traveled throughout the state campaigning for the Democratic candidate, Martin Van Buren, who ultimately lost to the Whig nominee, William Henry Harrison.

As his legislative career progressed, Johnson's oratorical skills became widely appreciated. Learning to modulate his voice, he forcefully asserted his opinions at strategic points during debates and campaign speeches. A veteran political observer described Johnson's style as "forcible and powerful, without being eloquent."

Johnson never learned to embrace self-deprecation, but often utilized humorous anecdotes to keep his speeches from becoming tedious. An opposition Whig leader grudgingly admired Johnson's skills as a debater: "A strong-minded man who cuts—when he does cut—not with a razor but with a case knife."

In 1841, Johnson successfully ran for a seat in the state Senate, winning the election by some 2000 votes. The newly elected Senator proved stubborn and independent, and was often a lightening rod for controversy. A strong proponent for the separation of church and state, he opposed daily prayers in the legislature. A local newspaper was outraged at his position, labeling Johnson as an "avowed infidel." Infidel was perhaps too harsh, but Johnson was not exposed to religion as a child, and failed to establish attachments to any church as an adult. Some observers speculated, at heart, Johnson was a deist.

Senator Johnson proposed elimination of the *Three-Fifths Rule*, utilized for apportionment of congressional districts, whereby each slave was counted as three-fifths of a white citizen. A newspaper headline excoriated him: "Senator J—An Abolitionist." In reality, Johnson was no Abolitionist, but realized revocation of the existing law would politically strengthen his native Eastern Tennessee, where the slave population was much smaller.

Johnson was named Chairman of the *Joint Select Committee on Laying out the State of Tennessee in Congressional Districts*. Utilizing this position of power, he was able to increase Democratic Party representation across the state.

Believing the people of East Tennessee had more in common with the citizens of adjacent mountainous states than the planter aristocracy that dominated much of the remainder of the Volunteer State, Johnson proposed the creation of a new state to be called *Frankland* (in honor of the name given to the area in the 18th century). The new state would have included East Tennessee and portions of Virginia, Western North Carolina, and Northern Georgia. Johnson's controversial proposal was ultimately voted down by the Tennessee legislature.

By the early 1840s, Andrew Johnson was the acknowledged leader of the East Tennessee Democratic political machine, and a prosperous, well-respected businessman. Few were surprised when his political ambitions shifted toward national office.

Chapter 6

He cut and slashed and tore big wounds

Andrew Johnson's successful election to the United States House of Representatives in 1843 came on the coattails of a mud-slinging campaign. Johnson's political enemies launched savage attacks, with a Whig newspaper editorialist labeling him as, "mean, corrupt, selfish, and notoriously reckless."

Now a confirmed Democrat, Johnson returned the fire, characterizing the Whigs as *elitists*, who favored the rich and powerful. On the campaign trail, he was quick to respond to unruly crowds.

"Only two creatures hiss in nature—one a viper, from the malignity of its own venom, and the other a goose, because of its stupidity," Johnson confronted a heckler.

Johnson won the 1843 election by a mere 547 votes, but, at age 34, was now a United States Congressman. After being elected to Congress, Johnson continued to manage his own business, but never again worked as a tailor. Over the course of the next 10 years, he was re-elected to the House of Representatives on 4 occasions.

Johnson traveled to Washington D.C. to join the 28th Congress, leaving his invalid wife, Eliza, in Tennessee. The new Congressman found lodging in a boarding home, and uncertain of his political future, did not purchase a home. His loneliness was partially lessened by the presence of his daughter, Martha, who was attending the Georgetown Female Seminary.

Johnson never assimilated into the Capitol City social scene, preferring to spend his idle hours in the Congressional Library, furthering his self-education. Consequently, he rarely patronized the theater or attended social galas.

In the mid 1800s, Washington D.C. was an unfinished city. Tracts of clear-cut timberland and low-lying swampland separated the scattered, ornate government buildings. The Capitol, White House, Treasury Building, and Patent Office were the only finished structures, and were separated by unpaved roads. Muddy city streets were often impassable during the rainy season, and filled with choking dust during droughts. The oppressive heat and humidity of summer were nearly unbearable, forcing many citizens to abandon the capitol city for more temperate climates.

Johnson began his congressional career among a notable cast of characters, who would leave their unique footprints on American history. Johnson's colleagues in the House of Representatives included Hannibal Hamlin (a future Vice-President), Stephen Douglas (a future presidential candidate), Alexander Stephens (the future Vice-President of the Confederacy), and a fiery Mississippian named Jefferson Davis (the future President of the Confederate States of America). Among Johnson's Senate contemporaries were James Buchanan (a future President), and the historical trio of Daniel Webster, John C. Calhoun, and Henry Clay, whose combined legislative skills and ability to forge compromises, delayed the inevitable war between the foes and proponents of slavery.

John Quincy Adams was in the midst of his seventeen-year career as a Massachusetts Congressman, marking the first and only time an ex-President had been elected to that legislative body. The tart-tongued Adams, sometimes called *Old Man Eloquent*, was never generous with praise, but nonetheless, was impressed with his colleague from Tennessee: "This young man, Johnson, appears to have great native ability."

At the time of Johnson's election to the House of Representatives, the Democratic Party held a majority of the seats. While many of his votes reflected the mainstream opinion of his party, Johnson remained fiercely independent, establishing an unfailing record of voting his conscience on each and every issue.

Johnson never forgot his impoverished past, and remained a dedicated advocate for the poor and the common laborers. He favored the working class (who were often called *mechanics*), and remained suspicious, and, at times, hostile toward the so-called *aristocracy*. Characterizing himself as a "plebian mechanic," Johnson clearly identified with tradesmen and small farmers: "If this country is to have an aristocracy at all, I want that aristocracy to be an aristocracy of labor, and an aristocracy of agriculture and mechanics."

Johnson remained frugal with the taxpayer's money, refusing to vote for non-essential appropriations. Among his dissenting votes were opposition to a pay raise for soldiers, federal funding for the newly established Smithsonian Institute, purchase of a monument to be erected at the gravesite of John Quincy Adams (who died in 1848, after collapsing during a congressional session), and the purchase of the official papers of former President, James Madison. Johnson's fiscal conservatism also extended to taxation, where he opposed levies on coffee and tea.

Disdainful of wealthy business interests, Johnson opposed the establishment of a *National Bank*. For the remainder of his congressional career, he would remain wary of placing excessive power in the hands of a single institution.

Perhaps Andrew Johnson's grandest dream was the enactment of a *Homestead Law*, whereby poor farmers could migrate to the developing territories and occupy unclaimed federal lands. Johnson firmly believed that land ownership would elevate the social and financial positions of impoverished Americans. On March 27, 1846, Congressman Johnson introduced the *Homestead Act*: "A Bill to authorize every poor man in the United States, who is the head of the family, to enter 160 acres of public domain, without money and without price."

"Pass this bill and you will make many a poor man's heart rejoice. Pass this bill, and their wives and children will invoke blessings on your head," Johnson proclaimed.

Opposed by Northern industrialists, and more notably, Southern plantation owners, neither of whom were eager to see wide distribution of land ownership, the Homestead Act passed the House, but was defeated in the Senate. A disappointed Johnson would be forced to wait several years before his dream would become a reality.

When debating a point of law or defending his position, Johnson was passionate, thin skinned, and, easily offended. Mississippi Congressman, Jefferson Davis, a proud and aloof West Point graduate, angered Johnson when he praised the skill of army engineers, contrasting them to the "common blacksmith or tailor." Johnson angrily confronted Davis on the floor of the House, defending the honor of the workingman.

Through the years, many politicians and newsmen would find themselves on the receiving end of Johnson's verbal assaults. A *New York Times* reporter described Johnson's oratorical style: "He cut and slashed and tore big wounds, and left something behind to fester and be remembered. His phraseology may be uncouth, but his views are easily understood, and he talks strong thoughts and carefully culled facts." That same reporter summarized a debate, where Congressman Johnson was "running his opponent through and through with a rusty, jagged weapon, chopping to mincemeat his luckless adversary."

In 1844, Johnson was forced to defend the honor of his family. After completion of the congressional session, he traveled to his native North Carolina to address rumors spread by a vitriolic newspaper editor. Johnson was able to disprove the allegation that he had been born an illegitimate son. However, another controversial claim proved accurate—Johnson's first cousin had indeed been hanged after committing murder in a barroom brawl.

Before leaving Raleigh, Johnson visited his father's grave in the potter's field. A simple stone slab, partially covered by weeds, marked the burial site of Jacob Johnson—a sad metaphor for the mudsill. At the same time, Johnson was proud to have vindicated his father's good name.

In the summer of 1844, Johnson attended the Democratic National Convention in Baltimore, serving as an alternate delegate. To the surprise of many, he spoke against the nomination of fellow Tennessean, James Polk. A staunch admirer of the famed Andrew Jackson, Polk was nicknamed *Little Hickory*, and had achieved notoriety in Congress, serving as Chairman of the Ways and Means Committee, Democratic Majority Leader, and Speaker of the House (he would ultimately become the only House Speaker ever elected President). In spite of Polk's many accomplishments, Johnson did not believe his colleague was the strongest presidential candidate, and readily shared his opinion with fellow convention delegates, sparking a long-standing conflict between the two Southern statesmen.

Polk ultimately captured the Democratic nomination without Johnson's support, and went on to win the presidential election. Johnson's failure to support Polk came back to haunt him. The new President often refused Johnson's requests for patronage, describing his fellow Tennessean as "vindictive and perverse in temper and conduct." Johnson was infuriated by Polk's grudge, and readily defended his independent and honorable choice during the nominating process. In spite of his personal differences with the newly elected President, Johnson supported Polk's decision to annex Texas and also backed the Administration's declaration of war against Mexico.

Overcoming the opposition of Tennessee's growing Whig Party, Johnson managed to win re-election four times, and served in the House of Representatives for ten consecutive years. On the campaign trail, he encountered harsh criticisms and outright slander, but ardently defended his populist agenda: "The aristocrats in the district know I am for the people." Historian, Ralph W. Haskins, summarized Johnson's five terms as a Congressman: "His record in the House of Representatives reveals him as a dissenter, often petty in dissent, a blunt man of principle, to whom compromise was almost invariably the wrong solution, and a verbal bludgeonist, who now and then showed a trace of demagogue."

While he was considered unbending and opinionated, Johnson's congressional colleagues grew to respect him. Carefully researching each and every legislative proposal, the Tennessee Congressman's tireless work on the House floor and in committees was readily acknowledged. Johnson's diligence was rewarded, when he was appointed Chairman of the *Committee on Public Expenditures*. In the spring of 1847, Johnson caught the eye of freshman Illinois Congressman, Abraham Lincoln, leading to a lasting bond between the two men.

During his tenure in the House of Representatives, Johnson warily eyed the growing conflict between the industrial North and the agrarian South. Southern cotton planters had grown dependent upon slave labor, and hoped to extend their agricultural interests to the Western frontier, where expanding territories would eventually be admitted as new states. Citing *States' Rights* as justification for constitutional limitations on Federal power, Southerners asserted that newly formed states should have the right to permit slavery, if a majority of the population supported it.

In contrast, Northerners were motivated by both moral and political concerns. Politicians in the Northeast and upper Midwest realized the addition of slave states, with their newly elected Representatives and Senators, would shift the balance of power in Congress, and would also reshape the electoral map for future presidential elections.

From a selfless perspective, many Northerners (and a select minority of Southerners) viewed slavery as an evil institution, giving birth to the *Abolitionist Movement*. Many slaveholders countered the Abolitionist's claims of moral superiority, by referring to Biblical references justifying slavery.

The publication of Harriet Beecher Stowe's *Uncle Tom's Cabin*, which vividly portrayed the evils of human bondage, ignited anti-slavery forces. A distinguished group of African Americans (including Frederick Douglas, Sojourner Truth, and Harriett Tubman) emerged on the national scene, giving voice to the cry for freedom. An impressive array of white Abolitionists (like William Lloyd Garrison, Alton Parker, and Elizabeth Cady Stanton) also called for an end to slavery.

As the 19th century neared its mid-point, prominent political voices entered the slavery debate. Massachusetts Congressman (and former President of the United States), John Quincy Adams, who "abhorred slavery," fought to lift the House of Representative's *gag rule* that prohibited consideration of anti-slavery petitions. Not surprisingly, Andrew Johnson opposed ending the gag rule.

In 1848, former President, Martin Van Buren, attempted to re-gain office by running as the candidate of the newly formed, anti-slavery, *Free Soil Party*. Van Buren's come-back proved unsuccessful, when he failed to earn a single electoral vote.

In 1850, Congress passed the *Fugitive Slave Act*, whereby U.S. Marshalls (instead of private bounty hunters) were authorized to chase down escaped slaves. Seven years later, the Supreme Court ruled in the *Dred-Scott* case that slaves were private property, rather than citizens. The impact of this new legislation coupled with the high court's edict crystallized northern opposition to slavery.

In the Deep South, an overwhelming majority of its white citizens adopted the mantra of States' Rights to justify the perpetuation of their established way of life. Ironically, less than one-quarter of white Southerners were actually slave owners. Of that twenty-five percent, less than half owned five or more slaves. The aristocratic plantation owners, who had long drawn the enmity of Andrew Johnson, were a small, but immensely powerful minority.

As the United States rapidly expanded toward the Pacific, the controversy over slavery steadily intensified. Southern leaders began to talk openly of secession, and the formation of a new, pro-slavery country.

Andrew Johnson adopted a separate, but untenable position from the Secessionists. While supporting the extension of slavery, Johnson was an unwavering advocate of the sanctity of the Union. He believed that slaves were private property and slavery should be allowed to expand, according to the will of the people in a given state. Johnson's justification of the perpetuation of slavery was grounded in his belief in the inferiority of the Negroes: "The black race of Africa are inferior to the white man in intellect—better calculated in physical structure to undergo drudgery and hardship;

standing, as they do, many degrees lower in the scale of gradation that expressed the relative relation between God and all that he had created, than the white man."

Johnson opposed the *Wilmot Proviso* (introduced on August 8, 1846, by Congressman David Wilmot), which would have prohibited slavery in territories recently acquired from Mexico. Johnson believed each state should decide the legality of slavery within its own borders. He also opposed legislation calling for the end of slavery and corresponding slave trade in the District of Columbia. Johnson ultimately introduced an unsuccessful bill to admit California as a free state, merge the District of Columbia into the slave state of Maryland, and adopt a stronger Fugitive Slave Law.

In 1849, Southerners grew apprehensive when Californians adopted a non-slavery Constitution and asked to join the Union as a free state. The prospect of a free California threatened the tenuous balance between free and slave states. Ultimately, the *Compromise of 1850*, proposed by Senator Henry Clay of Kentucky, cooled the Secessionists' fire. Clay's bill admitted California as a free state, prevented the prohibition of slavery in the *New Mexico Territory* (precursor to the states of New Mexico and Arizona, as well as Southern Nevada), banned slave trade (but not slavery) in the District of Columbia, and enforced the Fugitive Slave Act (requiring the return of runaway slaves, even if they were captured in free states).

When President Millard Fillmore signed the Compromise of 1850 into law, he proclaimed the legislation to be the "final settlement" to the conflict over slavery. In reality, the new law only intensified the passions of Northern Abolitionists.

With the exception of the provision banning slave trade in the District of Columbia, Johnson found the Compromise of 1850 acceptable. Along with a majority of his colleagues, Johnson voted the law into existence, temporarily easing tensions between the North and South.

Andrew Johnson enjoyed his career in the House of Representatives, but looked forward to recesses, when he could return home.

Expanding his business interests and enjoying continued financial success, Johnson purchased *The Spy*, a Greeneville newspaper, and purchased a larger home.

The ten-room house, known as *The Homestead*, was a block over and a block and a half down from his tailor's shop and previous residence.

While not elegant, Johnson's two-story brick home, which fronted Main Street, was attractive and stately, with a wrap-around porch on the side and back of both floors.

A comfortable overstuffed chair sat in front of the parlor fireplace, adjacent to a table stacked with Johnson's favorite books. In his downstairs bedroom, Johnson kept a picture of his beloved wife, Eliza, on the wall above his bed. In her upstairs bedroom, a sickly Eliza had her own *invalid chair* (akin to a modern day recliner). There were additional bedrooms for Johnson's children and grandchildren, as well as a formal dining room and a basement kitchen.

The polished plank floors and marbleized paneled walls provided the house with an understated dignity. The backyard garden boasted rose, currant, and gooseberry bushes, as well grapevine trellises and an aspen tree. Two weeping willow trees, allegedly transplanted from a location near Napoleon's grave, helped frame the periphery of the garden.

Andrew Johnson's idyllic life was disrupted by political storm clouds, which threatened his future in Congress. By 1852, the Whigs had gained control of the Tennessee state legislature, providing lawmakers with an opportunity to redraw Johnson's 1st Congressional District. As a result of this legislative *Gerrymandering*, Johnson's home district was suddenly populated by a much larger bloc of Whig voters.

In a biblical flourish, Johnson saw the handwriting on the wall: "I have no political future—my political garments have been divided, and upon my vesture, do they intend to cast lots." After a decade as a Congressman, Johnson avoided certain defeat, when he chose not to seek re-election.

At the end of 1853, Andrew Johnson retired from Congress and returned to Tennessee. Johnson's enemies, who were gloating over his political demise, would soon learn that they had underestimated the former mudsill.

Chapter 7

I will never desert them

The life of a retired Congressman did not suit Andrew Johnson. Even though the Whig Party controlled the Tennessee state legislature, Johnson remained popular among working-class citizens, earning the nickname, *Mechanic Statesman.* In 1853, he decided to take his case to the people of Tennessee, announcing his candidacy for the governorship. Adding fuel to the election year fire, Johnson's opponent, Gustavus Henry, was the Whig legislator who had orchestrated the Gerrymandering of the former Congressman's legislative district. Johnson's image as a self-educated tailor appealed to working-class voters, and he was elected Governor by a narrow margin of 2050 votes.

On October 17, 1853, the forty-four year-old Johnson was sworn into office. Emblematic of his bond to the common man, Johnson walked the streets of Nashville on the day of his inauguration, rather than travel in an ornate carriage.

The new Governor was gracious in his inaugural address, calling for a return to true Democratic principles: "Democracy is a ladder, corresponding in politics, to the spiritual one that Jacob saw in his vision—one, up which all, in proportion to their merit, may ascend." Johnson also expressed appreciation for the common man: "They have, so far, never deserted me, and, God willing, I will never desert them." Johnson's inaugural address would be remembered as his *Jacob's ladder speech*, promoting equality for all men—as long as they were white.

During the Antebellum Era, the Tennessee Governor's elective term was only two years, and gubernatorial powers were constitutionally restricted. The Governor was prohibited from issuing vetoes, and most state officials were elected by the legislature. Among his limited constitutional duties, Johnson was empowered to pardon prisoners and oversee certain public institutions, like the Bank of Tennessee and the state penitentiary.

The Whig-controlled legislature was disinclined to follow most of Governor Johnson's recommendations. Johnson made the most of his opportunities to govern, and was pleased when legislation was passed, adopting a uniform system for weights and measures. He was also able to persuade lawmakers to appropriate funds for the purchase of books for public libraries—a cause near and dear to the self-educated politician. Johnson recommended successful passage of the *Common School Bill*, which raised taxes and doubled appropriations to public schools. The Governor was delighted when the legislature authorized the purchase of Andrew Jackson's estate (*The Hermitage*, located near Nashville). As expected, Johnson continued to oppose governmental regulation of individual rights, as evidenced by his opposition to Prohibition.

Johnson readily utilized those powers allocated to him, and frequently pardoned convicted criminals. Believing *commoners* were often more severely punished, compared to their more affluent counterparts, the Governor readily commuted harsh sentences. Johnson also objected to hard labor as a method of punishment, believing such policy unfairly targeted the poorer prisoners. Later in his political career, Johnson would show similar mercy when dealing with treason cases.

During his tenure as Governor, Johnson lived alone at the Nashville Inn, while Eliza and his younger children remained in Greeneville. Isolated from his family, Johnson used his idle time to read and study.

Johnson remained notoriously thin-skinned, overreacting to slights, both real and perceived. After being harshly criticized by a Whig opponent, the Governor challenged the man to a duel.

Fortunately, a mutual acquaintance brokered a peaceful resolution, preventing bloodshed.

Johnson exploited every opportunity to showcase his bond with the working-class voters of Tennessee. After receiving a hand-forged set of fireplace irons from the Governor of Kentucky (who also happened to be a skilled blacksmith), Johnson reciprocated with a gift of his own—a hand-sewn suit of clothes.

In spite of his minority status as a Democratic Governor in a Whig-dominated state, Johnson remained popular with the people. In 1855, he decided to seek re-election for a second term.

The Whig Party soon joined forces with the former *American Party*, who had christened themselves as the *Know-Nothings*. The Know-Nothing Party was noted for its prejudice against Catholics and foreigners—when asked about party philosophy, members were instructed to answer that they "know nothing." In spite of his own racism, Johnson denounced the bigotry of the upstart party: "Show me the dimensions of a Know Nothing, and I will show you a huge reptile, upon whose neck the foot of every honest man ought to be placed."

The combined parties hoped to thwart Johnson's re-election, and even resorted to the use of threats. Prior to a campaign stump speech in a heavily occupied Whig district, Johnson heard rumors that he would be assassinated by a group of Know-Nothings. On the day of his scheduled address, the Governor entered the crowded hall, alone, and walked to the platform. Removing a pistol from his coat pocket, Johnson placed the weapon on the table in front of him: "Fellow citizens, it is proper, that when free men assemble for the discussion of important public matters, that everything should be done—in order. I have been informed that part of that business is the assassination of the individual who has the honor of address-ing you. I suppose, therefore, that this is the first business in order, and this is the proper time to proceed."

Placing his hand on the pistol, Johnson eyed the hushed crowd: "Gentlemen, it appears that I have been misinformed. I will now pro-ceed to address you on the subject that has called us together." The speech continued without incident, and Johnson was re-elected for a second term.

During his governorship, Johnson endured a series of misfortunes. In addition to Eliza's continued battle with tuberculosis, Johnson's son, Charles, drifted deeper into alcoholism, unresponsive to the interventions of family and friends.

On the night of April 13, 1856, a fire broke out at the Nashville Inn. Awakened from a deep sleep, the Governor assisted a distraught female guest out of the burning building. Hidden beneath his pillow was $1,200.00 in cash, which was destroyed by the flames.

In early 1857, Johnson traveled by train to deliver an out-of-state speech. While passing through Georgia, the locomotive derailed, sending the Governor's car tumbling down a sixty-foot embankment. The impact of the crash crushed Johnson's right elbow, leaving him with a painful, permanent injury.

Throughout his four years as Governor, Andrew Johnson remained an ardent racist. In order to justify the institution of slavery, Johnson declared that slaves in America occupied a more privileged position than their counterparts in Africa. While he deplored prejudice against the less affluent, Johnson characterized the black race as "an inferior type of man, incapable of advancement."

In 1857, Johnson decided not to seek re-election as Governor. Instead, he campaigned on behalf of his Democratic successor, Isham Harris. Much to Johnson's delight, the Democrats also won control of the state legislature from the Whigs.

In his final legislative address, Governor Johnson proposed a conservative agenda, including abolition of state banks and promotion of "hard money" (gold and silver instead of greenbacks). Johnson's devotion to his party pleased the newly elected Democratic legislature, which rewarded him with unanimous election to the United States Senate.

Chapter 8

It is treason, nothing but treason

When Andrew Johnson was sworn into office in the Senate on December 7, 1857, he announced that he had "reached the summit of my ambition." The rise from Alderman to United States Senator had been a remarkable feat for the self-educated tailor. However, Johnson's claim that he had fully sated his ambition was less than genuine.

The freshman Senator found Washington D.C. a much different place than it had been at the start of his first congressional term, 14 years earlier. The population of the Capitol City had swelled to 250,000, and the infrastructure of the federal government was firmly entrenched. Two new wings had been added to the Capitol Building to provide office space for Congressmen and Senators.

Once again, Eliza remained in Tennessee, forcing Johnson to live alone in a rented room at the Saint Charles Hotel, on the corner of Pennsylvania Avenue and Third Street. During his tenure in the Senate, Eliza made only one trip to Washington to visit her husband.

While serving in the Senate, Andrew Johnson's fiscal philosophy remained distinctly *Conservative*. Proving his commitment to frugality, he proposed elimination of congressional franking (post-marking) privileges. Johnson also opposed the *Transcontinental Railroad*, considering it a wasteful expenditure. After a confrontation with Johnson over the railroad issue, Mississippi Senator, Jefferson Davis, lamented that his relationship with his Tennessee colleague "had never been pleasant."

Consistent with his reputation as an independent thinker, Johnson voted his conscience on pending legislation, proudly proclaiming: "I am no party man, bound by no party platform, and I will vote as I please." While considered a maverick by many of his colleagues, Johnson's dedication to his legislative duties led to his appointment as Chairman of the *Committee to Audit and Control the Contingent Expenses.* He also served on the influential *Committee on the District of Columbia.*

Johnson continued to press for passage of a Homestead Act, introducing such legislation on December 22, 1857. The proposed bill again met opposition from some Northerners (who were not inclined to promote an agrarian society) and a vast majority of the Southern aristocracy (who did not want land suitable for plantations to be taken over by small farmers). While his Homestead Bill managed to pass both houses of Congress, it was vetoed by President James Buchanan, who was desperately trying to placate Southern slave owners. Johnson was disheartened when sectional conflicts derailed his dream legislation: "If the Ten Commandments were to come up for consideration, somebody would find a Negro in them somewhere, and the slavery question would be raised."

During Johnson's four-year congressional hiatus, the regional conflict over slavery had intensified. In 1854, the *Kansas-Nebraska Act,* sponsored by Illinois Senator and Democratic presidential aspirant, Stephen Douglas, was passed by Congress. The new law repealed the Missouri Compromise of 1820, and divided the Nebraska Territory into two separate territories (Nebraska and Kansas), allowing residents to vote whether or not slavery would be legal in those two future states. Proponents of slavery subsequently settled into Kansas, waging bloody civil war against anti-slavery forces, in what would become known as *Bleeding Kansas.* Fearing slavery would surely spread if put to the vote of the people, a powerful cadre of Northern politicians coalesced to form the Republican Party.

The battle lines between pro and anti-slavery factions in the House and Senate were now sharply delineated. As the Whigs and No-Nothings faded from history, the Republicans and Democrats emerged as the only major political parties. The Republican Party became home for an impressive array of anti-slavery leaders, including Senators Ben Wade of Ohio, William Seward of New York, and Lyman Trumbull of Illinois, along with Representatives Thaddeus Stevens of Pennsylvania, and Owen Lovejoy of Illinois.

The Democratic Party boasted its own formidable cast of pro-slavery lawmakers, including Senators Jefferson Davis of Mississippi, Robert Toombs of Georgia, and James Mason of Virginia, as well as Representative Roger Pryor of Virginia. The rhetoric of the mostly Southern, pro-slavery forces evenly matched that of their Northern opponents.

The verbal war on Capitol Hill eventually culminated in violence. On May 19, 1856, Massachusetts Senator, Charles Sumner, openly ridiculed his South Carolina colleague, Andrew Butler (one of the pro-slavery authors of the Kansas-Nebraska Act). Sumner attacked Butler for supporting pro-slavery forces in Kansas, where bloody civil war raging, and accused the South Carolinian of taking "a mistress, though ugly to others, is always lovely to him—though polluted in the sight of the world, is chaste in his sight—I mean the harlot, slavery." Sumner added insult to injury by mocking Butler's stroke-induced speech difficulties.

Three days after Sumner lambasted Butler, South Carolina Representative, Preston Smith Brooks (who also happened to be Senator Butler's cousin) entered the Senate chambers and accosted the Massachusetts statesman. Brooks savagely beat Sumner with a cane, until the hapless Senator was bloodied and unconscious.

Critically injured, Sumner was unable to resume his senatorial duties for several months after the brutal attack. In the wake of his assault on Sumner, Brooks resigned his House seat, explaining that he "meant no disrespect to the Senate of the United States." Congressman Brooks was hailed as a hero in the South, while Northerners labeled him a barbarian. A defiant Brooks maintained that he never meant to kill Sumner, or he would have used a more lethal weapon.

Andrew Johnson anxiously observed the escalating regional conflict, but remained hopeful a compromise could be reached.

Like the majority of Southerners, he supported the Supreme Court's Dred-Scott decision, whereby slavery was guaranteed constitutional protection. Johnson, however, occupied a lonely middle ground, by advocating both *States' Rights* and *Union Solidarity*. While he questioned the right of the federal government to dictate the legality of slavery within individual states, Johnson firmly believed that secession was unconstitutional. An avid States' Righter, Johnson supported the Kansas-Nebraska Act and Fugitive Slave Law, but was careful to point out he was not part of the Southern *slavocracy*. When all was said and done, Johnson's untenable position isolated him from Northerners and Southerners, alike.

The conflict between North and South neared its boiling point in October of 1859, when a fiery Abolitionist named John Brown led a raid against the Army Arsenal at Harper's Ferry, Virginia. With an attack force of 16 white men, 4 freed blacks, and 1 fugitive slave, Brown set his sights on the 100,000 rifles and muskets stored at the arsenal, hoping to initiate a widespread slave insurrection. Brown's men were eventually overwhelmed by military force (the Marines were led by Colonel Robert E. Lee, who would later achieve fame as the Commander of the Confederate Army), and the captured Abolitionist was convicted of treason and sentenced to hang. In his last written communication, the gallows-bound prisoner offered a dire prophecy: "I, John Brown, am quite certain that the crimes of this guilty land will never be purged away but with blood."

Brown's failed assault on Harper's Ferry convinced many Southerners that secession was the only means to protect their established way of life. While opposed to secession, Johnson nonetheless condemned Brown as "a sanguinary assassin, red with blood," who had been driven to violence by "Abolitionist propaganda."

As the 1860 Presidential election approached, the Democratic Party was in chaos. Andrew Johnson expressed interest in the presidential nomination and sent his older sons, Charles and Robert, along with a political strategist, Sam Milligan, to the party convention in Charleston, South Carolina. Johnson subsequently received Tennessee's delegate votes in each of the thirty-six deadlocked ballots.

The convention grew contentious over the adoption of a federal *slave code* (statutes governing the already limited freedoms of slaves) in U.S. territories. Delegates from the lower South supported this platform proposal, while the upper South opposed the slave code. When the measure was voted down, delegates from Alabama, Arkansas, Florida, Louisiana, Mississippi, South Carolina, and Texas marched out of the convention hall. The remaining delegates adjourned the Charleston convention, reconvened in Baltimore, and nominated Illinois Senator, Stephen Douglas, for President.

As the nominee of the traditional Democratic Party (aka *Northern Democrats*), Douglas proposed popular sovereignty to determine the legality of slavery. Douglas had long been considered the Democratic Party's savior, but his opposition to the Dred-Scott ruling made him an unacceptable presidential candidate in the eyes of Southern voters. Vice-President John Breckinridge was nominated by the *National* or *Southern Democrats*, who threatened secession. Former Tennessee Congressman, John Bell, was selected as the nominee of the *Constitutional Union Party* (a group of former Southern and Border State Whigs and a handful of displaced Know-Nothings).

In contrast, the Republicans were solidly behind their nominee, Abraham Lincoln, who vowed to keep the Union intact. During his unsuccessful bid to unseat Stephen Douglas in the 1858 Illinois Senatorial race, Lincoln offered a now famous forewarning: "This government cannot endure, permanently, half-slave and half-free." Lincoln had also made public his views on the immorality of slavery: "As I would not be a slave, so I would not be a master."

Andrew Johnson maintained his Democratic loyalty by supporting Breckinridge, but was less than optimistic about his party's chances. One day before the General Election, he predicted that Lincoln would win the presidency, thereby triggering the secession of most Southern states. With the future of the country in serious doubt, Johnson defiantly affirmed his own position: "As for me, I will be found standing by the Union."

Southern Democrats were alarmed at the prospect of Lincoln winning the presidency against the fractured Democratic Party. A

Georgia Congressman warned his colleagues of the ramifications: "We will never submit to the inauguration of a *Black Republican* as President. I speak the sentiment of every Democrat on this floor from the state of Georgia."

Southern foreboding became reality when Abraham Lincoln was elected President in November of 1860, by a narrow plurality (39.65 percent of the total vote). Lincoln carried 18 *Free* States, winning 1,865,593 popular votes and an electoral majority (180 votes). Breckinridge won all 11 states in the Deep South, earning 848,356 popular votes (72 electoral votes). Bell carried three of the *Border* States (529,906 popular votes and 39 electoral votes). Stephen Douglas, the one-time rising star of the Democratic Party, managed to carry only one state (Missouri). In spite of his 1,382,713 popular votes, Douglas won only 12 electoral votes, leaving his national political career in shambles.

After Lincoln's election, Andrew Johnson was in political no-man's land. As a *Union Loyalist*, he was estranged from the vast majority of Southerners, while his defense of slavery alienated him from many Northerners.

Soon after Lincoln's election, the country began to unravel. On December 3, 1860, lame-duck President, James Buchanan, delivered an ineffectual address to Congress. While he believed secession was unconstitutional, Buchanan declared that it was also unconstitutional for the federal government to use force against the states to prevent them from withdrawing from the Union. Johnson openly criticized President Buchanan's failure to take a firm stance against the Southern Rebels. Congress appointed two special committees, hoping to forge some sort of an agreement between pro and anti-slavery foes, but the vast majority of Southerners were in no mood to compromise.

Johnson made a vain effort to intervene, proposing bold constitutional revisions—direct, popular vote election of the President and Vice President (abolishing the Electoral College), as well as the appointment of Supreme Court Justices for twelve-year terms (rather than life appointments). Johnson also recommended establishment of a *Senate Committee of Thirteen* to develop a `amendment specifying the division of territories into slave and non-slave states: "I believe it is the imperative duty of Congress to make some effort to save the country from impending dissolution . . ."

Speaking on Senate floor, Johnson argued against the legality of secession: "It is treason, nothing but treason, and, if one state, upon its own volition, can go out of this Confederacy without regard to the effect it is to have upon the remaining parties to the compact, what is your government worth?" Johnson accused Southern politicians of maneuvering "in an attitude of levying war against the United States." Citing the words of Andrew Jackson, Johnson hoped to stir feelings of national patriotism: "The Federal Union, it must be preserved."

"I intend to stand by the Constitution as is, upon a compliance with all its guarantees," Johnson asserted, "It is the last hope of human freedom."

Johnson's denunciation of Secessionists was decidedly similar to the rhetoric of his hero, Andrew Jackson: "I would have them arrested and tried for treason, and, if convicted, by eternal God, they should suffer the penalty of the law at the hands of the executioner."

Johnson's pro-Union stance was greeted with indignation in his native South. North Carolina Governor, John Ellis, labeled the Tennessee Senator "a traitor to his section." Another North Carolinian, Senator Thomas Bragg, alleged that Johnson, having been treated "with little or no respect" by his Southern congressional colleagues, had retaliated by siding with the North. In his home state, Johnson was burned in effigy by a mob of Memphis Secessionists.

Outside the Deep South, Andrew Johnson was transformed into a hero of sorts. The *Chicago Tribune* championed his Union-solidarity speech to the Senate as "a stunning blow at the treason of the seceding states." Johnson received letters of support from throughout the country—one correspondent paid him the ultimate compliment, characterizing the Union Loyalist as "the Old Hickory of this age."

While believing the institution of slavery should be protected, Johnson warned friend and foe alike: "God forbid that this country shall ever be in a servile or civil war—I shall stand by the Constitution."

In December of 1860, Johnson was the only Southern lawmaker to warmly greet the President-Elect, when Lincoln visited Capitol Hill to pay a courtesy call on the Congress. On that day, Lincoln quietly endured the heated rhetoric of the so-called *fire-eaters*, like Jefferson Davis, Judah Benjamin, and Robert Toombs, who denounced the Union and advocated the right of secession.

On December 20, 1860, South Carolina made the first move toward dissolution, when its legislature voted to secede from the Union. In the next six weeks, Mississippi, Florida, Alabama, Georgia, Louisiana, and Texas followed suit. In February of 1861, Tennessee Governor, Isham Harris, called for a *Secession Convention*. The state legislature opted to place the question before a popular vote in a special election. Tennessee voters subsequently rejected the proposal by a large margin. Johnson applauded the results, and accused the fire-eaters of behaving as unreasonably as the Abolitionists.

Gallant but unsuccessful efforts were made to preserve the Union. On February 4, 1861, a *Peace Convention*, chaired by former President, John Tyler, convened in Washington, D.C. Tyler, a native Virginian, hoped to stem the tidal wave of secession, but the delegates were unable to reach an agreement acceptable to either side. After the failed Peace Convention, the former President returned to his home state and urged Virginia's citizens to join the Secessionist tide. Tyler was later elected as a Representative to the *Confederate Congress*, but died in January of 1862, before he was able to attend his first legislative session.

In late February, Congress passed a joint resolution calling for an amendment to the Constitution guaranteeing slavery in states where it already existed. The state of hostility between politicians from the North and South, however, doomed the resolution.

On February 8, 1861, the newly formed *Confederate States of America (CSA)* held its inaugural convention in Montgomery, Alabama. As the cornerstone of newfound independence, the Confederate Constitution preserved the institution of slavery. The convention delegates chose former Mississippi Senator, Jefferson Davis, as President of the CSA, and elected the fire-eating Georgian, Alexander Stephens, as Vice-President.

Johnson loudly denounced the newly-formed Confederacy in a March 2nd speech: "Show me those who make war on the Government and fire on its vessels, and I will show you a traitor. If I were President of the United States, I would have all such arrested, and if convicted, by the eternal God, I would have them hung!"

On March 4, 1861, six-feet, four-inch Abraham Lincoln towered over most of his contemporaries on the speaking platform erected on the steps of the Capitol Building. Sharply focusing his somber, gray eyes, Lincoln attempted to reassure rebellious Southerners during his inaugural address: "I have no purpose, directly or indirectly, to interfere with the institution of slavery. I believe I have no lawful right to do so, and I have inclination to do so."

At the same time, the new President offered an unmistakable warning that "no state upon its own mere motion can lawfully get out of the Union." Near the end of his address, Lincoln placed the onus of responsibility on the Secessionists: "In your hands, my dissatisfied fellow countrymen, and not in mine, is the momentous issue of *civil war* ..."

While Andrew Johnson was encouraged by the words of the new President, the vast majority of Southerners believed Lincoln's promises were too little and too late. In anticipation of Confederate hostilities, President Lincoln made a firm decision to protect all federal properties within the Deep South. Fort Sumter, in the Charleston, South Carolina harbor, was among the military instillations Lincoln ordered provisioned.

Louisiana native, General P. G. T. Beauregard, commander of the Confederate military forces defending Charleston, eyed Fort Sumter with much anticipation. The gray clad Confederates, convinced that "one Rebel could lick a hundred Yankees," were itching for a fight. At 3:30 a.m. on April 12, 1861, General Beauregard sent a message to the Union Commander, Major Robert Anderson. In a strange twist of fate, Anderson, a Union loyalist from Kentucky, had been one of Beauregard's instructors when the Confederate General was a cadet at West Point. Beauregard's message to his former teacher was blunt: "Surrender at once, or be fired upon in one hour from now."

Anderson failed to heed the surrender order, and Confederate batteries began firing on the island fort at 4:30 a.m. After 33 hours of bombardment from over 4000 artillery shells, Major Anderson was forced to surrender. With the fall of Fort Sumter, President Lincoln succinctly remembered: "And, the war came."

After the Confederate attack on Fort Sumter, Andrew Johnson traveled to Tennessee, with hopes of keeping his home state in the Union. A hostile reception awaited him, as angry mobs confronted his inbound train. At one stop, an intruder invaded Johnson's passenger car and pulled the Senator's nose. After Johnson drew his pistol, a railroad official intervened and prevented bloodshed.

Johnson immediately went on the attack, warning his constituents that secession would lead to anarchy and the formation of "petty little governments, with a little prince in one, a little potentate in another, and a republic somewhere else." On April 27, 1861, Johnson addressed a crowd near Knoxville, condemning secession, and reminded his fellow citizens that Tennessee's foremost statesman, Andrew Jackson, had always been a proponent of Union solidarity. While Johnson spoke, a company of Confederate soldiers tried to interrupt the meeting. The ranking Confederate Army officer forced his way into the room and ordered Senator Johnson to halt his address.

"Captain, I have been a Democrat all my life, and accustomed to the rule of the majority. If the majority of this crowd wants me to continue, I will, regardless of you and your company," Johnson defiantly answered. Unwilling to risk further confrontation, the Rebel officer exited the building.

Undeterred by Confederate hostility, Johnson continued his tour of the state, arguing against secession. In Jonesboro, he denounced his one-time ally, Isham Harris, who was now Tennessee's rabid, Secessionist Governor: "Are the people of Tennessee to be handed over to the Confederacy, like sheep in the shambles?" The Jonesboro crowd, like others, booed Johnson. The Loyalist Senator was denounced as a "damned traitor" by many of his fellow citizens.

Johnson's efforts to halt the rebellion were in vain. On June 8, 1861, voting for a second time, Tennesseans approved an *Ordinance of Secession* (by a vote of 81,000 to 47,000), and formally joined the Confederate States of America. Johnson felt a measure of vindication, when his fellow citizens in East Tennessee voted to remain in the Union, outnumbering the Secessionists by a vote of 33,000 to 14,000.

As a confirmed Union Loyalist, Johnson realized it was too dangerous to remain in Tennessee. On June 12, 1861, he departed Greeneville, never dreaming that he would be unable to return to his hometown for nearly eight years. Johnson left behind his wife, two daughters, and six year old son, Andrew, Jr. Johnson's travel party was actually fired upon by Confederate sympathizers before they were outside the borders of Tennessee.

Nine days later, Johnson arrived in Washington D.C., and discovered that he was the only Southern Senator to have remained remain loyal to the Union. Though demonized by fellow Southerners, the courageous and defiant Johnson was hailed as a hero by other Union Loyalists. The *New York Times* praised him as "the greatest man of the age."

Soon after returning to Congress, Johnson delivered a three-hour speech on the Senate floor. Voicing support for special presidential *War Powers*, he defended Lincoln's suspension of the right of *habeas corpus*. Johnson maintained that the President was acting to defend the Constitution: "It is not Lincoln, but Davis who is overthrowing our government and making of it despotism."

After his Senate speech, Johnson received letters from citizens throughout the country, praising his courage and patriotism. In Tennessee, however, the name Andrew Johnson was vilified. Supporters of the Confederacy harassed and imprisoned Union Loyalists in Tennessee. Johnson's son, Charles, who was actively recruiting volunteers to join the Union Army, was forced into hiding to avoid imprisonment.

Johnson defended the honor of his hometown loyalists: "Rewards are out for my capture. I am told officers, with warrants, are hunting me down, but I am no runaway, no fugitive—except a fugitive from tyranny, and I thank God that the country in which I live is with me. On the 8th of this month, the county of Greene, Tennessee, gave a 2000- vote majority against the odious, diabolical, nefarious, hell-born, and hell-bound doctrine called secession." In July of 1861, Johnson and Kentucky Senator, John Crittenden, co-sponsored a resolution proclaiming that the Civil War was solely about *preserving* the Union, rather than *subjugating* the South or *destroying* slavery.

Concerned about the safety of his family and friends back home, Johnson unsuccessfully lobbied President Lincoln to launch an invasion of East Tennessee. The Union Army was already spread thin, and lacked experienced military leaders, preventing immediate liberation of Johnson's homeland. Exiled in Washington D.C., and unable to return home for the foreseeable future, Johnson was sadly philosophical: "I have not the means of writing to my own family, and do not expect to have any means of doing so until this nefarious rebellion is put down."

To cope with his mounting anxiety and depression, Johnson focused on work. He was appointed as one of three members of the *Senate Joint Committee on the Conduct of the War* (aka the *Wade Committee*), and joined his colleagues in exhaustive questioning of Union Generals, pushing them to more aggressively prosecute the war. Johnson remained particularly impatient with the Union Army's continued reluctance to invade East Tennessee.

When General Ulysses S. Grant captured Fort Henry and Fort Donelson in western Tennessee, the Confederate Army was forced to abandon much of the state, including the capitol city of Nashville. After Grant's twin triumphs, President Lincoln summoned Andrew Johnson to the White House.

"Andy, I am most grateful for the work you have been doing on the Wade Committee. Your presence is an inspiration to others. In spite of this, I want you to take on another assignment," Lincoln explained.

"Yes?" Johnson inquired.

"You know, of course, that Grant has reduced the two forts in western Tennessee. This frees that area of Tennessee from the Rebels, and it seems that this is just the moment to establish federal control, and give new spirit to the loyal men and women in that state who have suffered so much."

Johnson silently nodded, as the President continued: "I want to appoint you as *Military Governor* of Tennessee, so that your voice can inspire the loyalists and near-loyalists in that border state."

With Tennessee no longer a part of the Union, Andrew Johnson had no Senate seat to defend in the forthcoming election. With no other political options available, the newly appointed Military Governor prepared to return home.

Chapter 9

I return to you with no hostile purpose

Abraham Lincoln considered lands captured by the Union Army as conquered territories, requiring strict military supervision. To that end, Andrew Johnson became the first appointed Military Governor. On March 4, 1862, Johnson received his official orders signed by Secretary of War, Edwin M. Stanton: "You are hereby appointed Military Governor of the State of Tennessee, with the rank of Brigadier General, and with authority to exercise and perform within the limits of the state, all and singular, the powers, duties, and functions pertaining to the Office of Military Governor (including the power to establish all necessary officers and tribunals and suspend the right of *habeas corpus*) during the pleasure of the President, or until the loyal inhabitants of the state shall organize a civil government in conformity with the Constitution of the Unites States." At the end of the proclamation, President Lincoln added a sentence in his own handwriting: "Upon your wisdom and energetic action, much will depend in accomplishing the result." In many respects, Tennessee, under the rule of a Military Governor, would serve as a test case for Lincoln's plans to administer post-war *Reconstruction* of the divided Union.

Throughout the country, Union Loyalists applauded Johnson's appointment. The *New York Tribune* termed the choice "eminently proper". His congressional career terminated by the Civil War, Johnson anxiously returned to his hostile home turf.

On March 11, 1862, Johnson arrived in Nashville, where he would live for the next three years, as the Civil War entered its bloodiest period. The newly appointed Military Governor soon received an abundance of hate mail from fellow Tennesseans—the writers used terms like "traitor, scum, vile, and wretch." He also endured more than his share of death threats.

Johnson held firm, writing to his wife: "I feel sometimes like giving up in despair, but this will not do. We must hold out to the end; this rebellion is wrong and must be put down, let cost what it may in life and treasure. I intend to appropriate the rest of my life to the redemption of my adopted home, East Tennessee, and you and Mary (Johnson's daughter) must not be weary. It is our fate, and we should be willing to bear it cheerfully. Impatience and dissatisfaction will not better it or shorten the time of our suffering."

Tennessee's Confederate Governor and Legislature fled to Memphis prior to the fall of Nashville, leaving Johnson as the sole authority in the capitol city. Unwavering in his devotion to the Union, Johnson attempted to reason with local citizens. On March 13th, the newly appointed Military Governor addressed a crowd of Nashvillians: "I return to you with no hostile purpose. I come with the olive branch in one hand and the Constitution in the other, to render you whatever aid may be in my power…" Privately, Johnson was less forgiving: "Traitors must be punished and treason crushed."

Johnson acted swiftly and firmly, seizing control of the *Bank of Tennessee*, impounding all court records, and taking charge of the railroads. He demanded that city government officials take an oath of allegiance to the United States. Those who refused were expelled and replaced by men loyal to the Union. The Mayor of Nashville, Richard Cheatham, was imprisoned for several weeks, before reluctantly agreeing to take the oath of allegiance. Governor Johnson was unyielding, to the point of arresting and incarcerating ministers who refused to take the loyalty oath or chose to preach pro-Confederate sermons. Citizens who openly criticized the Union were arrested and held without trial.

In May of 1862, Nashville held local elections, ostensibly to establish a loyalist government. When a known Secessionist was elected to a judgeship, Governor Johnson allowed the man to assume office, arrested him for disloyalty, and appointed a rival candidate to the post.

Johnson further utilized his wartime powers to muzzle the press. Pro-Confederate newspapers, like the *Nashville Times*, were forced to shut down their presses. Johnson also levied a tax on the wealthiest Secessionists to support war related expenses.

Nashville's safety was imperiled when Rebel forces, led by Generals Nathan Bedford Forest and John Morgan Hunt, threatened attack. Governor Johnson took charge of the defense of Nashville, erecting breastworks on the periphery of the city and rationing food to prevent starvation. Johnson angrily threatened to destroy the homes of Secessionists, if the Confederate Army invaded, and also vowed to execute any citizen attempting to surrender. During the height of the crisis, Johnson often slept in his office in the Capitol Building. From atop the Statehouse dome, he carefully observed the position of both Union and Confederate troops outside of Nashville.

While Johnson was determined to defend the state capital, the Union Army Commander in West Tennessee, General Don Carlos Buell, talked of abandoning the beleaguered capitol city. Exasperated with Buell's seemingly defeatist attitude, Johnson wrote the Secretary of War, Edwin Stanton: "May God save my country from some of the Generals that have been conducting the war." As the Confederate Army drew closer to the city, Governor Johnson confided his fears and frustrations to Colonel Dwight Moody, a Union Army evangelist, who was conducting a crusade among the Federal troops defending Nashville.

"Moody, Buell is a traitor. He is going to evacuate the city, and, in forty-eight hours, we will all be in the hands of the Rebels," Johnson proclaimed.

The military officer/preacher could not calm the agitated Governor.

"Moody, can you pray?" Johnson finally asked.

"Why, yes, that is my profession as a minister of the Gospel," Moody answered.

"Well, then, I want you to pray right now," Johnson ordered, before dropping to his knees.

Moody delivered an impassionate prayer for the safety and security of Nashville, before Johnson concluded with an enthusiastic, "Amen!"

"Moody, I feel better," Johnson said, placing his hand on the evangelist's shoulder, "I don't want you to think that I have become a religious man. I do believe in Almighty God. And, I do believe in the Bible, and I say I'll be damned if Nashville shall surrender!"

Perhaps through divine intervention, Confederate forces besieging the capitol city finally withdrew in early November of 1862. Suffering through the agonizing pain of kidney stones, Johnson nonetheless remained steadfast in his defense of Nashville. A New York newspaper reporter, assigned to Tennessee, wrote about his unwavering leadership: "The cool and determined demeanor of Governor Johnson is the admiration of all."

Johnson's frustration with the Union Army leadership in western Tennessee lessened when General Buell was transferred out of the area and the command was assigned to William Rosecrans. For the duration of the war, Nashville remained under Union control.

Though he ruled with an iron hand, Governor Johnson was generally compassionate toward the enemy. He commuted the death sentences of many captured Confederate soldiers, believing that most enlisted men were the pawns of the plantation owners who controlled the Confederacy. Johnson maintained that the Civil War was being fought to preserve the Union as opposed to ending slavery: "Damn, the Negroes—I am fighting these traitorous aristocrats—their masters!"

Later, when pressed to explain the interrelationship between the rebellion and slavery, Johnson hinted that if the Confederate States would voluntarily end slavery, the Civil War could be ended: "If you persist in forcing the issue of slavery against the Government, I say, in the force of Heaven, 'Give me my Government and let the Negroes go!'" Predictably, Johnson was unable to mask his racism, even in the light of emancipation: "Before I would see this government destroyed, I would send every Negro back to Africa, disintegrated and blotted out of space." Moreover, he offered no promise of racial equality: "The whites are and will continue to be masters of this country."

Johnson set an example by freeing his own slaves in 1863. He immediately offered them employment as house servants, and most readily accepted his offer.

An interesting interlude between future Presidents of the United States occurred when Union Army General, Ulysses S. Grant, visited Governor Johnson in Nashville. During a joint public appearance, the shy and taciturn Grant witnessed Johnson's impassioned address: "…It was long, and I was in torture while he was delivering it, fearing something would be expected of me in response. I was relieved; however, the people assembled having heard enough."

Slowly, the Civil War turned in favor of the Union. Numerical superiority favored the North—the Union had more fighting men and industrial capacity to support the war effort, as well as more railroads to transport soldiers and materials. At the beginning of the war, the North was crisscrossed by 22,000 miles of railroad, compared to just 9000 miles in the Deep South. The Confederate states had only 18,000 industrial factories, while the Union boasted 110,000 such facilities. Consequently, the Rebels were forced to fight a war of attrition, especially after France and England, unwilling to alienate the United States, refused to join forces with the Confederacy.

On September 22, 1862, Abraham Lincoln took the first step toward ending slavery and depriving the enemy of its vital agrarian manpower, by issuing the *Emancipation Proclamation*; which freed slaves in the Confederate states (it did not free slaves in states that had not seceded—a common historical misconception). Lincoln defended the justness and appropriateness of the decree: "I never in my life felt more certain that I was doing right."

As Military Governor of Tennessee, Andrew Johnson believed that Tennessee was a *reconstituted* member of the Union, and convinced President Lincoln to exclude his home state from the list of those considered to be in rebellion. As such, when the Emancipation

Proclamation took effect on January 1, 1863, Tennessee was the only Confederate state exempted from the decree.

In February of 1863, Johnson traveled to Washington D.C. to consult with President Lincoln concerning the progress being made in Tennessee, before embarking on a pro-Union speaking tour in the Northeast and Midwest. Johnson's fiery speeches placed blame for the Civil War squarely on the South: "The time has come to teach the South and the North that institutions do not exist here that are more powerful than the government, itself. Has slavery a right to agitate the government and shake it to its center, and then deny to the government the privilege to agitate slavery?"

Andrew Johnson endured considerable personal turmoil during the course of the Civil War. East Tennessee remained in Confederate hands much longer than the rest of the state, and when Rebel forces seized Johnson's house, Eliza, and young son, Frank, were forced to leave town within thirty-six hours. Eventually, mother and son made their way through enemy lines, and settled in Indiana, where the climate was thought to be more favorable to Eliza's tuberculosis.

Johnson shared his bitterness in a letter to a friend: "The Confederates went to my home when my wife was sick; my child, eight years old, consumed with consumption. They turned her and the child into the streets, converted my house, built with my hands, into a hospital and barracks. My servants, they confiscated. It was with much suffering that my wife and little boy were able to reach the house of a relative, many miles distant. Call you this *Southern rights*? If so, God preserve me from another such affliction."

Angry Rebel troops defaced Johnson's home with graffiti. On the wall in Eliza's bedroom, a Confederate invader wrote: "Andrew Johnson, the old traitor." Johnson's portrait, which hung in the parlor, was rescued by a benevolent Greenevillian, who kept it hidden and undamaged for the duration of the Civil War.

Further tragedy befell the family in 1863, when the Johnson's son, Charles, an assistant surgeon with the Middle Tennessee Union Calvary, was killed after falling from his horse. Charles' death occurred while Andrew was in Washington D.C., and the grieving father was unable to attend his son's funeral.

While he remained a racist at heart, Andrew Johnson's position on slavery evolved as the war progressed. The Governor publicly supported the Emancipation Proclamation, and denounced slavery as a "cancer on society". At the request of President Lincoln, Johnson allowed some 20,000 black Tennesseans to enlist in the Union Army.

On December 3, 1863, President Lincoln issued an *Amnesty Proclamation* (aka the *Louisiana Plan*), which allowed the re-establishment of state governments across the South, after ten percent of the voters signed an amnesty oath. Lincoln's so-called *Ten Percent Plan* made no provision of suffrage for freed slaves, which the President believed would have to be mandated by a constitutional amendment.

On January 21, 1864, the Tennessee state legislature passed a resolution condemning slavery, and asked to be readmitted to the Union. Since the Emancipation Proclamation did not apply to the state, Governor Johnson pressured lawmakers to adopt a statewide amendment repealing slavery. Thus, Tennessee became the only Confederate state to *voluntarily* abolish slavery.

Johnson also granted amnesty to Confederate sympathizers. On January 26, 1864, the Governor issued an oath to be affirmed by Tennessee voters: "I solemnly swear that I will henceforth support the Constitution of the United States and defend it against the assaults of all enemies."

As Military Governor of Tennessee, Andrew Johnson exercised broad dictatorial powers and established a loyalist state government. He defied the Secessionist majority, risking his life and endangering the well being of his family. His actions led to the abolition of slavery in Tennessee, and prepared the state for readmission to the Union.

Johnson also earned the respect and admiration of Abraham Lincoln, who was carefully plotting his re-election strategy.

Chapter 10

Vice-President

In order to prosecute the war to a successful conclusion and reunite the Union, Abraham Lincoln needed to win re-election in 1864. Once the Civil War ended, the task of post-war *Reconstruction* promised to be a formidable challenge, and Lincoln believed that he could bridge the sectional divides. To promote an image of unity and make it easier for pro-war Democrats to support Lincoln, the Republicans christened themselves as the *National Union Party*.

When the new party met for its national convention, it was a fore-gone conclusion that Lincoln would head the ticket, but the issue of the vice-presidency had yet to be settled. Many Republicans feared that the incumbent, Hannibal Hamlin, a native of Maine, was too radical, and might alienate voters in conservative Border States.

Lincoln was aware of Andrew Johnson's courage and deter-mination, and the Tennessean's reputation as a man of action ap-pealed to the President's political pragmatism. Even though he was a Southerner and a Democrat, a Loyalist like Johnson would likely be popular among Northern voters. Johnson was also a favorite of working-class voters, particularly Irish Catholics, who appreciated his long-standing denunciation of religious prejudice. In short or-der, Johnson became the front runner for the *Republican/National Union* vice-presidential nomination.

In June of 1864, convention delegates nominated Abraham Lincoln for a second presidential term. The motion to nominate Hamlin for Vice-President, however, was soundly defeated. When the selection of Lincoln's running mate was opened to the delegates,

Andrew Johnson won the nomination handily, gathering 494 out of 520 votes. When he learned of his nomination, Johnson was enthusiastic and somewhat bemused: "What will the aristocrats do with a *rail-splitter* for a President and a *tailor* for Vice-President?"

Johnson's nomination was well received in the Northern and Border states. An editorialist for the *Louisville Press* wrote: "The nomination of Andrew Johnson, of Tennessee, for Vice-President will be responded to everywhere with the expression of heartfelt satisfaction by the loyal people of the country. No man has labored more earnestly in the cause of the government than he has. His name is inseparably connected with the history of this mighty struggle for the maintenance of the Union and free government." Abraham Lincoln welcomed Johnson's nomination with characteristic understatement: "Andy Johnson, I think, is a good man."

On June 25, 1864, Johnson's face appeared on the cover of *Harper's Weekly*. The photograph, taken by the famed Matthew Brady, was the vice-presidential candidate's first nationwide exposure.

Some Republicans, however, were not pleased with the choice of Johnson as Lincoln's running mate. Pennsylvania Representative and ardent Abolitionist, Thaddeus Stevens, led a chorus of lawmakers who wanted to punish the South for their role in defending and perpetuating slavery. Stevens and his cohorts formed a coalition that earned the moniker *Radical Republicans*.

"Can't you find a candidate for Vice-President in the United States, without going down to one of those damned Rebel provinces to pick one up?" Stevens loudly protested. In a private conversation with Lincoln, Stevens even was blunter: "Mr. President, Andrew Johnson is a rank demagogue, and, I suspect, at heart, a damn scoundrel."

When word reached Nashville of Johnson's nomination, many local citizens were relieved, believing the readmission of Tennessee to the Union would be painless; an expectation not shared by the remaining Confederate states. Amidst the booms of celebratory cannon fire, Governor Johnson addressed his supporters: "The Convention announced and confirmed a principle not to be disregarded—it was that the right of secession and the power of a state to place itself out of the Union are not recognized. By taking a nominee from one of the rebellious states, the Union Party declared its belief that the rebellious states are still in the Union—that their loyal citizens are still citizens of the United States."

In July of 1864, four months before the election, President Lincoln faced a showdown of sorts with the Radical Republicans in Congress. Senators Benjamin Wade of Ohio and Henry Winter Davis of Maryland introduced legislation establishing criteria for readmission of Confederate states into the Union. The *Wade-Davis Bill* added a punitive feature to Lincoln's proposed *Ten Percent Plan*, requiring a *majority* of voters in each state to swear allegiance to the United States and further declare they had *never* supported the Confederacy. Under those proposed terms, most white Southerners would have been disqualified from voting. The Wade-Davis Bill passed both houses of Congress on July 2, 1864, but President Lincoln refused to sign it into law, employing the *pocket veto*.

Lincoln justified his opposition to the Wade-Davis Bill, indicating he was not yet committed to a single plan of Reconstruction. The President also asserted that Congress did not have the authority to abolish slavery, which would have to be ended by constitutional amendment. In response to Lincoln's pocket veto, Radical Republicans in Congress issued the *Wade-Davis Manifesto*, proclaiming that Congress had "absolute authority" to deal with the rebellious Confederate states.

"There is no government in the Rebel States, except for the authority of Congress," Senator Davis declared.

Andrew Johnson supported Lincoln's opposition to the Wade-Davis Bill, believing there should be a clear system of checks and balances between the branches of the federal government. Johnson also defied the tradition of non-participation by vice-presidential candidates during nationwide elections, when he made speeches in Tennessee and neighboring states. A fiery Johnson reminded an Indiana crowd that the sanctity of the Union was absolute: "Fellow citizens, and I trust I shall be permitted to call you such, not withstanding I reside in a state that was said to have rebelled and separated itself from the United States, for I hold the doctrine that a state could not secede."

While never fully abandoning his belief in the inferiority of the black race, Johnson had nonetheless become an outspoken advocate for the abolition of slavery. He believed the end of slavery would free both blacks and whites, creating a mixed race class of commoners, and would dampen the political and economic influence of the white aristocracy. Johnson was careful to clarify his position; Negroes should be given a chance to establish their place in freed states, under the auspices of a white man's government.

Johnson's popularity in the black community increased, as newly freed slaves flocked to hear the words of the Great Emancipator's running mate. On October 24, 1864, Johnson addressed a group of freed blacks on the steps of the Capitol Building in Nashville: "Looking at this vast crowd of colored people, and reflecting through what a storm of persecution and obloquy they are compelled to pass, I am almost induced to wish that, as in the days of old, a Moses might arise, who should lead them safely to their promised land of freedom and happiness.

"You are our Moses!" the enthusiastic crowd responded

"God, no doubt, has prepared somewhere, an instrument for the great work He designs to perform in behalf of the outraged people, and, in due time, your leader will come forth. Your Moses will be revealed to you," Johnson declared.

"We want no Moses, but you!" the freedmen responded.

Caught up in the enthusiasm of the moment, Johnson's subsequent remarks exceeded the scope of his intentions: "Well, then, humble and unworthy as I am, if no other better shall be found, I will indeed be your Moses, and lead you through the Red Sea of war and bondage, to a fairer future of liberty and peace."

Johnson's *Moses Speech* drew praise from Northern Abolitionists. Many Radical Republicans came to believe the Tennessee Loyalist would join them in advocating a policy of *harsh* Reconstruction. In reality, Johnson's commitment to civil rights would never match the bold rhetoric of his Moses Speech.

On the first Tuesday in November, the Lincoln/Johnson ticket swept to victory, gathering 55 percent of the popular votes, and besting Democratic candidate, George McClellan, by an electoral margin of 212 to 21. Lincoln won all but 3 states, and the Republican Party won majorities in the House of Representatives (149 to 42) and the Senate (42 to 10). McClellan, the former Union Army General, who Lincoln had removed from command for not aggressively pursuing the enemy, had promised to continue slavery as an inducement for ending the Civil War. In a stinging rebuke to the one time General, Lincoln won 70 percent of the Union Army vote. In Andrew Johnson's home state of Tennessee, Lincoln won by nearly 25,000 votes, even though Confederate soldiers denied pro-Union voters access to the polls in a number of precincts.

Andrew Johnson, the former Mudsill and devoted Loyalist had been elected Vice-President of the United States. His electoral triumph was yet another chapter in a remarkable rag to riches story.

In January of 1865, the Tennessee Constitutional Convention ratified the 13th Amendment, forever abolishing slavery. Vice-President Elect Johnson sent President Lincoln a congratulatory telegram: "Thank God that the tyrant's rod has been broken."

Chapter 11

Andy ain't a drunkard

In the early months of 1865, Vice-President Elect Johnson was stricken with typhoid fever, leaving him weak and debilitated for several weeks. Johnson contacted President Lincoln and asked if he might skip the inaugural festivities in early March (the presidential inauguration date would not be moved to January until the 1940s), and remain in Tennessee until his health returned to normal. The President and his Cabinet, who were eager to display solidarity, insisted the new Vice-President be on hand for the official start of Lincoln's second term.

Not yet fully recovered from his illness, Johnson reluctantly left Nashville by train, accompanied by his personal physician. The night before the inaugural ceremony, Johnson emerged from his hotel room sick bed to attend a party in his honor, where he consumed a good bit of wine.

March 4, 1865 dawned cold, wet, and windy. Wearing a new black frock coat, silk vest, and doeskin pants, Johnson waited at his hotel for the outgoing Vice-President, Hannibal Hamlin, to escort him to the Capitol Building. During the short carriage drive to Capitol Hill, Johnson, sick and perhaps hung over, experienced cold chills and dizziness. Arriving at the Capitol Building, the Vice-President Elect was escorted to Hamlin's Office, where he hoped to rest a bit.

"Mr. Hamlin, I am not well, and need a stimulant. Have you any whiskey?" Johnson inquired. Hamlin, a confirmed teetotaler, immediately dispatched an aide to purchase a bottle of liquor.

As he waited for the inaugural ceremony to begin, the Vice-President Elect consumed three tumblers filled with whiskey, hoping to lessen the chills and steady his nerves: "I need all the strength for the occasion I can have." In short order Johnson was not only sick, but also intoxicated.

At noon, Hamlin and Johnson entered the stuffy, crowded Senate chambers, arm in arm, finding their way to the speaker's dais. President Lincoln sat on the front row with his Cabinet officers to witness the formal swearing in ceremony for his new Vice-President. Hamlin spoke first, thanking his colleagues for their kindnesses during the preceding four years. Turning to Johnson, Hamlin introduced his successor: "Is the Vice-President Elect now ready to subscribe to the oath of office?"

Johnson stepped to the podium, drunk and more than a little confused. Eyeing the hushed gallery, he delivered an ill-advised and disjointed address: "Senators, I am here today as the chosen Vice-President of the United States, and, as such, by the constitutional provision; I am made the presiding officer of this body. I, therefore, present myself here, in obedience to the high bequests of the American people, to discharge a constitutional duty, and not presumptuously to thrust myself in a position so exalted. May I, at this moment—it may not be irrelevant to the occasion—advert to the workings of our institutions under the Constitution, which our fathers framed and George Washington approved, as exhibited by the position in which I stand before the American Senate, in sight of the American people? Deem me not vain or arrogant, yet I should be less than a man, if, under the circumstances, I were not proud of being an American citizen, for today, one who claims no high descent, one who comes from the ranks of the people, stands by the choice of a free constituency, in second place in this government."

The stunned observers were puzzled by his rambling monologue. Secretary of the Navy, Gideon Welles, turned to the Secretary of the War, Edwin Stanton: "Johnson is either drunk or crazy."

"There is evidently something wrong," Stanton whispered in reply.

"I hope it is sickness," Welles lamented.

Hamlin tugged on the Vice-President Elect's coattail, trying to bring a quick end to his successor's disastrous speech. Johnson, however, was not finished: "I will say to you, Mr. Secretary Seward, and to you, Mister Secretary Stanton, and to you Mr. Secretary… Who is the Secretary of the Navy?"

A whispered voice informed Johnson of the forgotten name: "And, to you, Mister Secretary Welles, I would say, you all derive your power from the people."

To the great relief of the assembly, Johnson finally concluded his twenty-minute speech, and recited the vice-presidential oath of office. He then kissed the Bible: "I kiss this book in the face of my nation of the United States."

Abraham Lincoln, who had awkwardly stared at the tops of his boots during Johnson's drunken performance, quickly exited the Senate chambers to take his oath of office on the Capitol's east portico. Before exiting the building, the President collared a federal marshal: "Do not let Johnson speak outside."

Former slave and ardent Abolitionist, Frederick Douglas, was among the invited guests to the inauguration. Observing the stern, unsmiling countenance of the new Vice-President, Douglas offered a grim prediction: "Whatever Andrew Johnson may be, he is not friend to our race."

Lincoln's second inauguration drew a crowd of 50,000. His inaugural address was brief; barely 700 words in length, but the eloquent message would be forever remembered. The President summarized his hopes for reconciliation: "With malice toward none, and charity for all, with firmness in the right as God gives us to see the right, let us strive to finish the work we are in, to bind up the nation's wounds, to care for him who shall have born the battle, and for his widow and orphan to do all which may achieve and cherish a just and lasting peace among ourselves, and with all nations."

After Lincoln's inaugural address, Vice-President Johnson asked a friend to take him to his hotel, where he returned to his sick bed. Dizzy and weak, Johnson was not yet fully aware of the implications of his drunken harangue.

Almost immediately, the Vice-President came under attack. The *New York Times* reported on his "shameful speech," characterizing it as "the most incoherent public effort on record." Johnson was characterized as a "drunken clown" by the *New York World*. Michigan Congressman, Zachariah Chandler, wrote his wife about the controversy: "The inauguration went off very well, except the Vice-President was too drunk to perform his duties, and disgraced himself and the Senate by making a drunken, foolish speech. I was never so mortified in my life. Had I been able to find a hole, I would have crawled through it, out of sight."

President Lincoln tried to dispel rampant rumors about his new Vice-President: "I have known Andy for many years. He made a slip the other day, but you need not be scared. Andy ain't a drunkard." Lincoln's assessment was accurate. Johnson, who had witnessed the ravages of alcohol abuse on two of his sons, was not an alcoholic. While fond of Tennessee bourbon, Johnson was never known to have been publicly intoxicated on any other occasion, in spite of rumors to that effect. The Inauguration Day debacle, however, tarnished Johnson's reputation, and his tenure as Vice-President began under the darkest of clouds.

Two days after the inaugural ceremony, Johnson presided over the opening day of the Senate session, before dropping out of sight. He spent the early days of his vice-presidency resting and recuperating at the Silver Spring, Maryland estate of Francis P. Blair. The affluent Blair, founder of the *Washington Globe* newspaper, also owned a four-story mansion on Pennsylvania Avenue, across the street from the White House (this dwelling would later serve as the official residence for visiting dignitaries, and eventually become known as the *Blair House*). Blair was among a group of influential citizens who founded the Republican Party, and his son, Montgomery, had served as Lincoln's first Postmaster General. During the controversial early days of his vice-presidency, the entire Blair family remained faithful to Johnson.

The Vice-President gradually emerged from his self-imposed isolation, hoping to regain the President's trust and confidence. On

April 9th, Johnson traveled to the newly liberated Confederate capitol in Richmond. The Rebel government had abandoned the city in the closing days of the war, and its deposed leaders were in flight, hoping to elude capture by Union troops. Johnson was shocked by the devastation; rubble, burned out buildings, ruined railways and bridges, barren farmland, and starving livestock littered the landscape. The depressing scene convinced Johnson that the civilian population in the South had suffered enough, and he concluded that all future punishments should be directed at military leaders and government officials, rather than the general populous. To the leaders of the former Confederacy, the Vice-President offered a terse warning: "Treason must be made odious; traitors must be punished and impoverished."

In contrast to Andrew Johnson's desire to punish Confederate leaders, Abraham Lincoln proposed leniency. Just two days after Jefferson Davis fled Richmond, President Lincoln traveled to the vanquished Confederate capitol. As Lincoln walked the streets of Richmond, he joyously proclaimed: "Thank God that I have lived to see this! It seems to me that I have been dreaming for four years, and now the nightmare is gone."

When a group of freed slaves knelt at Lincoln's feet and kissed his boots, the President gently admonished them to kneel only to God, but reassured them about the future: "As long as I live, no one shall put a shackle on your limbs."

During his tour of fire-ravaged and debris-ridden Richmond, Lincoln came upon the presidential mansion, located on the corner of 12th and Clay Streets, which now served as headquarters for the *Union Army of Occupation*. Entering the abandoned *Confederate White House*, Lincoln settled into Jefferson Davis' office chair and reflected on the country's troubled past and promising future.

Born ten months and one-hundred miles apart in Kentucky, Abraham Lincoln and Jefferson Davis had charted separate career courses before fate placed them as the heads of warring nations. Davis was now on the run, hoping to join up with the fragmented remains of the Confederate Army, or at worse, escape to Mexico.

Lincoln's attitude toward his vanquished rival was surprisingly nonchalant. A few days earlier, the President had confided to his aides that if Davis escaped "unbeknown" to him, he would not object. As for the remainder of the civilian and military leaders of the Confederacy, Lincoln was inclined to "let 'em up easy."

On April 9, 1865, Confederate General, Robert E. Lee, surrendered his army to Union General, Ulysses S. Grant, ending the Civil War. The famed military leaders met at Appomattox Courthouse, Virginia, where Grant, adopting the pattern set forth by President Lincoln, tendered generous terms of surrender.

After laying down their rifles and signing paroles, Confederate soldiers were allowed to keep their side arms, horses, and uniforms. Grant informed Lee that his troops were free to return to their homes without being held as prisoners of war or facing punishment as traitors.

While President Lincoln and General Grant demonstrated a capacity for forgiveness, Andrew Johnson did not fully embrace their benevolence. In early April, the Vice-President spoke at a Republican rally outside the Patent Office. When Johnson mentioned Jefferson Davis by name, listeners angrily denounced the former Confederate President: "Hang him! Hang him!" Consumed by the crowd's passion, Johnson proclaimed: "Yes, I say hang him *twenty* times!"

The Radical Republicans in Congress grew increasingly frustrated with President Lincoln's attitude of forgiveness. Consequently, many Republican lawmakers were reassessing their opinions of the new Vice-President. While Johnson might well have been an intemperate drunkard, many Radical Republicans were encouraged by his threats to punish the traitorous Rebel leaders. Even so, as long as Abraham Lincoln was President, Johnson's opinion carried little weight.

Less than a week later, John Wilkes Booth altered the course of history.

Chapter 12

Johnson, we have faith in you

Abraham Lincoln died at 7:22 a.m. on Saturday, April 15, 1865, some nine hours after being shot by John Wilkes Booth. In the rear bedroom of the Petersen house, across the street from Ford's Theatre, Secretary of War, Edwin Stanton, stared at the lifeless body of his Commander-in-Chief: "Now he belongs to the ages."

After Lincoln's body was taken to the White House for an autopsy and burial preparations, the Cabinet met in the back parlor of the boarding home and drafted a formal written statement informing the Vice-President of Lincoln's death. The letter was hand delivered to Andrew Johnson at his hotel, along with the Cabinet's recommendation that he take the oath of office as soon as possible. Major General Henry Halleck visited Johnson at the Kirkwood House and warned him not to leave the hotel without an armed guard.

At 10:00 a.m., Chief Justice Salmon Chase administered the presidential oath to Johnson in the parlor of his hotel suite. The Secretary of War, Secretary of the Treasury, Attorney General, four Senators, one Congressman, and a handful of Johnson's friends crowded into the room to witness the historic moment. After repeating the oath, the new President kissed the Bible and addressed the small group: "Gentlemen, I must be permitted to say that I have been almost overwhelmed by the announcement of the sad event which has so recently occurred. I feel incompetent to perform duties so important and responsible as those which have been so unexpectedly thrown upon me. As to an indication of any policy which may be pursued by me in the administration of the Government, I have to say that must be left for development as the Administration progresses. The message or declaration must be made by acts as they transpire. The only assurance that I can now give is reference to the past. The public life, which has been long and laborious, has been founded, as I in good conscience believe, upon a great principle of right, which lies at the basis of all things. The best energies of my life have been spent in endeavoring to establish and perpetuate the principles of free government, and I believe the Government in passing through its present perils will settle down upon principles consonant with popular rights more permanent and enduring than heretofore. I must be permitted to say, if I understand the feelings of my own heart, that I have long labored to ameliorate and elevated the condition of great mass of American people. Toil and honest advocacy of great principles of free government have been my lot. Duties have been mine; consequences are God's. This has been the foundation of my political creed, and I feel that in the end, the Government will triumph and these great principles will be permanently established. In conclusion, let me say that I want your encouragement and countenance. I shall ask and rely upon you and others in carrying the Government through its present perils. I feel in making this request that it will be heartily responded to by you and all other patriots and lovers of the rights and interests of a free people."

"You are President. May God support, guide, and bless you in your arduous duties," Chief Justice Chase proclaimed. Secretary of the Treasury, Hugh McCullough, remembered Johnson as "calm and self-possessed" before and after taking the oath.

At noon, President Johnson presided over his first Cabinet meeting, and asked all Lincoln Administration appointees to remain in office. William Hunter was appointed as the Acting Secretary of State, until the critically wounded William Seward could resume office. Back home in Tennessee, Johnson's daughter, Martha, wrote to her father: "The sad, sad news has just reached us, announcing the death of President Lincoln. Are you safe, and do you feel secure?"

Andrew Johnson was the first person in American history to become President following the murder of his predecessor. The American people quickly embraced their new leader, seeking reassurance after Lincoln's assassination. On April 18th, the *Chicago Tribune* reported that Lincoln had led the country "out of Egypt and across the Red Sea of Civil War," and predicted that Johnson would subsequently "drive out the Hittites and Amorites." Charles Sumner, the Radical Republican Senator from Massachusetts, took the biblical reference to an even higher plane, terming the assassination of Lincoln as the "judgment of the Lord."

Religious metaphors aside, the new President faced a daunting challenge in a country torn asunder by 4 years of savage fighting. Over 600,000 Americans had been killed during the Civil War— 360,000 on the Union side and 260,000 Confederates, equivalent to 1 out of every 50 people residing in the United States. Viewing the war in relation to its root cause, for every 6 slaves freed, 1 soldier had died. Nearly 500,000 men were wounded in combat, adding to the catastrophic casualty count. To better understand the magnitude of the 260,000 Confederate deaths, the combined American fatalities sustained in the Revolutionary War, the Mexican-American War, the Spanish-American War, World War I, the Korean War, and the Vietnam War totaled 280,000. Andrew Johnson knew first hand of the tragedy, having lost his son and a son-in-law during the war.

The South had been hit particularly hard, and its infrastructure, including transportation, industry, and agriculture, was devastated. In 1860, prior to the onset of the war, the South had produced 5,000,000 bales of cotton. By 1865, output had plummeted to 300,000 bales. Confederate currency was nearly worthless, and inflation rates in major Southern cities topped 9000 percent.

Incredibly, 1 in 4 Southern males of military service age were killed during the war. Upon returning home, many Confederate soldiers were too debilitated to work on their farms or in their shops. In 1866, the state of Mississippi appropriated 20 percent of its budget for the purchase artificial limbs for combat veterans.

Reconstruction of the war-ravaged former Confederacy was the foremost issue facing President Johnson. Would he punish the

South as he had done during his Military Governorship of Tennessee, or would he "let 'em up easy" as Lincoln had promised?

The first three weeks of the Johnson presidency were overshadowed by the country's grief over Lincoln's death. The mourning process began while Lincoln's body lay in a mahogany coffin atop a black-draped catafalque in the East Room of the White House.

On the April 19th, designated as a *National Day of Mourning* for the slain President, Andrew Johnson joined 600 mourners in the East Room, positioning himself just opposite from the main entrance, standing at attention in front of his predecessor's open coffin. A close friend, Preston King, and former Vice-President, Hannibal Hamlin, stood on either side of the new President as 3 clergymen, including Lincoln's own minister (Reverend Phineas D. Gurley) delivered eulogies. The funeral service lasted nearly 2 hours, during which time Revered Gurley intoned: "It was a cruel, cruel hand, that dark hand of the assassin, which smote our honored, wise, and noble President, and filled the land with sorrow..."

After the White House funeral service, Lincoln's casket was carried by a horse-drawn caisson to Capitol Hill. The slain President's riderless horse followed the caisson, along with some 5,000 mourners, who marched down Pennsylvania Avenue. Thousands more lined the streets amid the sounds of muffled drumbeats and tolling church bells.

For 36 hours, Lincoln's body lay in state in the Capitol, where the walls and statues were draped in black (excluding the one honoring George Washington). Nearly 25,000 people, both black and white, passed through the rotunda to view Lincoln's body. The slain President was the second person in history to lay in repose in the Capitol rotunda—Kentucky Senator, Henry Clay, one of Lincoln's heroes, had been the first individual afforded that honor.

On April 21, 1865, Abraham Lincoln departed Washington for the final time. The mournful echo of the locomotive's whistle signaled a final goodbye, as the special funeral train began a 1,645-mile, circuitous trip back to Illinois. For 13 days, mourners bunched along the rail beds for a glimpse at Lincoln's flag draped coffin, as the train chugged through Maryland, Pennsylvania, New York, Ohio, and Indiana. The train also carried the body of the late President's son; Willie Lincoln, who had died 3 years earlier at age 11, had been temporarily interred in the family crypt of Supreme Court Clerk, William T. Carroll, in Washington D.C.'s Oak Hill Cemetery.

The new coach that transported the bodies of father and son back home had been completed just two months earlier. Christened the *United States*, the railcar housed a state room, dining room, and drawing room, which were finished with oak and walnut trim and silk upholstery, none of which Lincoln had lived to appreciate. With a picture of the late President mounted on the cowcatcher, the funeral train, which consisted of a single locomotive and eight cars, retraced the path (in reverse order) taken by Lincoln from Illinois to Washington, after he was elected President in 1860.

Lincoln's open casket was displayed for several hours each time in various government buildings along the way (including Philadelphia's Independence Hall and New York's City Hall), where solemn crowds paid their final respects to the *Great Emancipator*. At the conclusion of the funeral procession, more than 1,000,000 Americans in 12 different cities had viewed Lincoln's open coffin. An additional 7,000,000 people viewed the train as it chugged through more than 400 cities and towns.

On May 4th, the bodies of Abraham and Willie Lincoln arrived in Springfield, Illinois, where they were interred at Oak Ridge Cemetery, just outside the city. Bishop Matthew Simpson conducted the graveside services, eulogizing the slain President: "Standing, as we do today, by his coffin and sepulcher, let us resolve to carry forward the work which he so nobly begun." Abraham Lincoln had finally been laid to rest, twenty days after his assassination.

From the start, Andrew Johnson was confronted with scurrilous rumors that he was behind the assassination of President Lincoln. In reality, there was no evidence implicating Johnson in the conspiracy. In fact, John Wilkes Booth had intended for the Vice-President to be murdered on the same night as Lincoln. Had George Atzerodt not lost his nerve and fled the Kirkwood House, Johnson might have been killed or gravely wounded.

President Johnson allowed Secretary of War Stanton to supervise the investigation into Lincoln's assassination and the attempted murder of Secretary of State Seward. Under Stanton's watchful eye, the military relentlessly pursued John Wilkes Booth and his co-conspirators. On April 26, 1865 thirteen days after the President's murder, Booth was cornered inside a burning tobacco barn, near Port Royal, Virginia. An overzealous Union Army soldier shot the accused assassin in the neck before he could surrender.

"Tell my mother I died for my country. I thought I did my best," Booth whispered, as he lay dying.

A vindictive Stanton saw no reason to treat Booth's body with any semblance of dignity. Accordingly, the Secretary of War ordered the corpse buried beneath the floor of the Washington Arsenal.

President Johnson, acting on the advice of his Attorney General, authorized a military commission to conduct the trial of Booth's alleged accomplices. David Herold (who was with Booth when he was shot and killed, and held Lewis Payne's horse during the Seward murder attempt), George Atzerodt (who conspired to murder the Vice-President), Lewis Payne (who brutally attacked Secretary of State Seward), and Mary Suratt (whose Washington D.C. boarding house was the alleged site of pre-assassination conspiratorial meetings) were the principal defendants. Doctor Samuel Mudd (who set Booth's broken leg after Lincoln's assassination), Edward Spangler (who held Booth's horse behind Ford's Theater), Samuel Arnold, and Michael O'Laughlin (both of whom were accused of conspiring with Booth to kidnap President Lincoln in March of 1865) were tried alongside the others.

In the weeks leading up to their trial, the accused were incarcerated at the *Old Penitentiary* at the Washington Arsenal. The prisoners were forced to wear padded canvas head bags to prevent attempts at suicide by banging their heads again the jail cell walls—the only openings in the hoods were at the mouth, to allow the defendants to eat and drink.

The seven-week trial was conducted on the third floor of the Old Penitentiary building. The defendants were prominently displayed, seated on a raised deck at one end of the courtroom. General Joseph Holt, Judge Advocate of the Army, served as the government's chief prosecutor, and a nine-member commission heard the testimony of hundreds of witnesses. A simple majority (five of nine commissioners) was all that was necessary for conviction, and a two-thirds vote (six of nine) could impose the death penalty. While the defendants were assigned counsel, they were denied the right of higher court appeal. In the end, only the President of the United States was empowered to commute their sentences.

On June 29, 1865, the trial concluded with the prosecutor's final summation; the defense counsel was not allowed to offer a response. The commissioners deliberated behind closed doors for two days, before finding all of the defendants guilty. Lewis Payne, David Herold, George Atzerodt, and Mary Suratt were sentenced to death. Mudd and O'Laughlin were sentenced to life at hard labor, while Spangler received a six-year prison sentence. As an historic footnote, a year later, the U.S. Supreme Court ruled that military trials of civilians were unconstitutional.

Five of the nine commissioners later signed a petition requesting that Mary Suratt's sentence be commuted to life imprisonment, in light of her age (fifty-two) and sex. On July 5th, Judge Advocate General Holt visited the White House to allow President Johnson to review the trial documents. By Johnson's recollection, Holt never mentioned Suratt's clemency petition, and placed it among the court documents in a way that made it easy for the President to miss it. Without delay, the President signed all four death warrants.

On July 6th, Mrs. Suratt's daughter, Anne, traveled to the White House to plead her mother's case. Johnson's aides prevented the grief stricken woman from seeing the President. Consequently, Johnson would forever claim that he never saw Suratt's clemency petition—a claim later disputed by both Holt and Secretary of War Stanton.

On July 7, 1865, 3,000 spectators gathered in the prison court-yard to watch the hangings of David Herold, George Atzerodt, Lewis Payne, and Mary Surratt. Facing the gallows, Payne remained unrepentant about his crime: "I believe it was my duty!" Suratt became the first woman ever put to death by the federal government. The executed prisoners were buried in plain coffins, adjacent to the gallows. For the accused, justice had been swift and deadly.

Out of respect for the widow of the slain President, Andrew Johnson did not occupy the White House offices or residence until Mary Todd Lincoln vacated the premises. Due to her fragile emotional state, Mrs. Lincoln did not accompany the bodies of her husband and son back to Illinois.

During the interim period, Samuel Hooper, an affluent Congressman from Massachusetts, allowed the new President to live in his house at the corner of 15th and H Streets. Meanwhile, Johnson conducted Cabinet meetings and other official business at the Treasury Building. Mrs. Lincoln did not leave the White House until May 23, 1865, six weeks after her husband's murder.

Tensions between the new President and former First Lady remained high. Mary Todd Lincoln sent numerous requests to President Johnson, demanding that government appointments be granted, per the presumed wishes of her deceased husband. Johnson, while granting most of the requests, ignored the widow on a personal level, and Mrs. Lincoln later complained that the new President never sent her a letter of condolence, nor did he visit her in the White House.

President Johnson oversaw the massive reduction in military manpower and resources in the months following the conclusion of the Civil War. In August of 1865, 641,000 Union troops were discharged from service, and by October of 1866, the regular army numbered only 54,000 men. At the conclusion of the war, the Union Navy employed 600 ships. By the end of 1865, only 115 vessels remained in service, with the remainder being sold or placed in dry dock.

The new Commander-in-Chief was confronted with widespread devastation across the Deep South, along with the challenge of promoting the sociopolitical future of 4,000,000 freed slaves. Blinded by racial prejudice, Johnson concluded that the vast majority of former slaves were not capable of understanding the electoral process and participating in governmental affairs. Unwilling to acknowledge the sacrifices of 180,000 black soldiers who had served in the Union Army, Johnson privately vowed that he would not see the South "trodden under foot to protect Niggers."

Accordingly, in direct opposition to the expressed wishes of the Radical Republicans in Congress, the new President opposed large-scale black suffrage. In fact, Johnson's yet undisclosed master plan was simply to return the country to its pre-war constitutional roots, excepting the abolition of slavery.

In the early days of his Administration, Johnson played his political cards close to the vest. Encouraged by the new President's bellicose threats against former Confederate leaders, many congressional Republicans assumed that Johnson would adopt much *harsher* Reconstruction policies than his predecessor. On Easter Sunday, two days after Lincoln's assassination, a group of Republican Senators met with Johnson in his temporary office at the Treasury Building. Senator Benjamin Wade, the ardent Massachusetts Abolitionist, was certain the new Commander-in-Chief was on the same political page: "Johnson, we have faith in you. By the Gods, there will be no trouble, now, in running the government."

Ohio Congressman, George W. Julian, was confident Johnson would side with the Radical Republicans: "Aside from his known tenderness to the Rebels, Lincoln's last public avowal, only three days before his death, of adherence to the plan of Reconstruction he had announced in December 1863, was highly repugnant... While everybody was shocked at his murder, the feeling was nearly universal that the accession of Johnson to the presidency would be a Godsend to the country." Wade, Julian, and other Radical Republicans, however, seriously misjudged Andrew Johnson's willingness to allow others to dictate the course of his future policies.

On April 21, 1865, General William T. Sherman and Confederate General, Joseph E. Johnstone, reached an armistice, ending all armed conflict in the eastern theater of the Civil War (the last battle of the war was actually fought in Texas, on May 13, 1865). Jefferson Davis and his Cabinet were still on the run, nineteen days after the fall of Richmond.

While Andrew Johnson felt sympathy for the average citizen in the South, he harbored intense animosity toward Confederate civilian and military leaders. On May 2nd, the new President posted a $100,000.00 reward for information leading to the capture of Jefferson Davis—the largest bounty in American history. Union soldiers apprehended Davis eight days later, near Irwinville, Georgia. The former Confederate President was taken to Savannah, where he was placed on a ship and transported to *Fortress Monroe* in Virginia.

The hexagonal fort, named for former President, James Monroe, was protected by thirty-foot tall granite walls, and surrounded by a moat. On May 12, 1865, Jefferson Davis began his imprisonment, and was largely deprived of even basic rights, including outside exercise and reading materials (newspapers included). Armed guards remained inside Davis' unheated cell, day and night, depriving him of any privacy or solitude, and the prisoner's incoming and outgoing mail was censored. The jailors routinely mocked their infamous prisoner, calling him "Jeffy, Rebel chieftain, and state prisoner."

A few days after his arrival at Fortress Monroe, the deposed Confederate President was forcibly restrained by several guards and placed in shackles. On May 29th, the *Richmond Times* featured a sensational headline: MR. DAVIS MANACLED. The negative publicity generated by the story soon forced Secretary of War Stanton to order removal of the prisoner's shackles.

When informed that he was a prime suspect in the conspiracy to assassinate President Lincoln, Davis offered the perfect defense, suggesting that his accusers ask Andrew Johnson if he would vouch for Davis' innocence: "He (Johnson), at least, knew that I preferred Lincoln to himself."

After learning of the assassination, the Confederate President had been dismayed, fearing Johnson would treat the South in a much harsher manner than his predecessor: "Certainly I have no special regard for Mr. Lincoln, but there are a great number of men of whose end I would rather hear than his. I fear it will be disastrous to our people, and I regret it deeply."

Initially, Davis was not allowed to speak to his guards, nor were they allowed to engage him in conversation. Ever so slowly, the prisoner's conditions improved, and in October of 1865, he was transferred to a private room in the interior of the fort.

Meanwhile, President Johnson received numerous letters from angry Northerners urging him to order the torture and execution of the former Confederate President. At the same time, Davis' wife, Varina, contacted influential politicians and journalists, pleading for her husband to receive better treatment and the right of due process. For the time being, Davis remained in limbo—unindicted and imprisoned.

In the early months of his presidency, both Northerners and Southerners misjudged Andrew Johnson. The President immediately advocated a *lenient* Reconstruction, similar to plan proposed by Abraham Lincoln. Johnson believed ratification of the 13th Amendment, abolishing slavery (passed by Congress on January 1, 1865), nullification of the *Secessionist Ordinances*, and repudiation of the Confederate debt were sufficient acts of repentance, and fulfilled the requirements necessary for readmission to the Union. When the Radical Republicans in Congress learned of Johnson's formula for Reconstruction, battle lines were drawn for an epic struggle between the Executive and Legislative branches of the federal government.

On May 23, 1865, Andrew Johnson reached the zenith of his popularity as President. That day, a victory parade and military review were held in the nation's capital, honoring Union military forces. Some 60,000 people lined Pennsylvania Avenue to watch the gallant, blue clad soldiers march past. Joined by a distinguished group of leaders, including General Ulysses S. Grant, and Secretary of War, Edwin Stanton, President Johnson stood atop a reviewing stand draped with battle flags and the Stars and Stripes. Each Army Corp commander saluted the President as they passed under his review. The *New York Times* reported the ceremony in great detail, declaring that Johnson was a man of "courage, sound moral judgment, and patriotism."

The victory gala was the last triumphant moment of Johnson's ill-fated presidency.

Chapter 13

I am for a white man's government in America

Abraham Lincoln's *Proclamation of Amnesty and Reconstruction*, issued on December 8, 1863, offered a full pardon to any Southerner willing to take a loyalty oath and accept the emancipation of slaves, excluding: 1. Civil or diplomatic agents or officials of the Confederacy; 2. Individuals who left United States judicial posts to aid the rebellion; 3. Confederate military officers above the rank of Army Colonel or Navy Lieutenant; 4. Members of the United States Congress who left office to aid the rebellion; 5. Individuals who resigned commissions in the U.S. Army or Navy, and afterwards aided the rebellion; 6. Individuals who treated prisoners of war in an unlawful manner.

Once ten percent of their eligible voters (as measured by 1860 voter registration rolls) had sworn loyalty to the Union, individual states could establish new governments, and send elected Representatives and Senators back to Washington D.C. to reclaim their abandoned congressional seats. However, Lincoln's Ten Percent Plan included no provision for black suffrage, which disconcerted the Radical Republicans in Congress.

Lincoln had firmly believed that emancipation would never gain a foothold in the Deep South if the federal government imposed harsh Reconstruction policies. He had been equally certain that the permanent abolition of slavery must come in the form of a constitutional amendment, rather than by congressional legislation. In July of 1864, President Lincoln had pocket vetoed the punitive Wade-Davis Bill, and proceeded to implement his own lenient plan. By early 1865, just prior to Lincoln's assassination, Presidential Reconstruction was already underway.

The Union-occupied areas of Arkansas, Louisiana, and Tennessee had already set up *Ten Percent Governments* at the time of Lincoln's assassination, but no plan had been established to deal with the four slave states that had not joined the Confederacy. Delaware, Kentucky, Maryland, and Missouri, along with newly formed West Virginia (established in 1863), did not fall under the umbrella of Lincoln's Emancipation Proclamation, and slavery remained legal in those states.

When Andrew Johnson was unexpectedly elevated to the presidency, the process of Reconstruction needed considerable clarification and specificity. Johnson wanted to move swiftly, and allow the former Confederate states to "renew their allegiance to the United States, and to assume their functions as states of the Union." In spite of his earlier bellicose rhetoric, the new President favored his predecessor's lenient approach to Reconstruction: "It has been my steadfast objective to escape from the sway of momentary passions, and to derive a healing policy from the fundamental and unchanging principles of the Constitution."

As the Military Governor of Tennessee, Johnson was accustomed to making unilateral decisions, unchallenged by the legislative branch of government. As President, he believed restitution of the Union should be wholly managed from the White House, without congressional interference. Six weeks after becoming President, Johnson summarized his view of the post-Civil War South: "There is no such thing as Reconstruction. These states have not gone out of the Union; therefore, Reconstruction is not necessary."

On May 29, 1865, not yet two full months in office, Johnson made the first move to expand *Presidential Reconstruction*. Without calling Congress into special session (lawmakers had adjourned on April 15th), Johnson issued an *Amnesty Proclamation* to the citizens of the former Confederacy: "I _____, do solemnly swear (or affirm), in the presence of Almighty God, that I will henceforth faithfully support, protect, and defend the Constitution of the Union of States, there under; and that I will, in like manner, abide by, and faithfully support all laws and proclamations which have been made during the existing rebellion with reference to the emancipation of slaves—so help me God." This Executive Order was similar to Lincoln's 1863 Amnesty Proclamation, which had technically expired at the conclusion of the Civil War.

Certain individuals were not eligible for amnesty: 1. Officials of the Confederate government and all military officers above the rank of Colonel in the Army and Lieutenant in the Navy; 2. Rebel soldiers or sailors educated at public expense at West Point or Annapolis; 3. Citizens who left their homes to pass through enemy lines to aid the Confederacy; 4. Governors of Confederate states; 5. Pirates who had preyed upon Union ships, or individuals who engaged in raids launched from Canada; 6. Individuals who voluntarily participated in the rebellion with a taxable property value greater than $20,000.00; 7. Individuals who had broken the December 1863 oath; 8. All persons previously excluded from amnesty in President Lincoln's 1863 proclamation.

The President, however, reserved the right to grant *special amnesty* to any person, at his personal discretion. The proclamation also extended formal recognition to the established Ten Percent state governments. Once a given state ratified the 13th Amendment (abolishing slavery), it was free to set up a reconstructed government without supervision from the federal government. Johnson appointed *Provisional Governors* for those states, until the reconstituted governments were fully functional.

The Amnesty Proclamation, which was unanimously approved by Johnson's Cabinet, made no mention of equal rights or black suffrage. The order also restored all properties (except for slaves) confiscated by the Union Army to their Southern owners. A prominent Southern newspaper summarized the President's actions: "Mr. Johnson had set his foot down against permitting Negroes having anything to do with putting the state governments in operation."

The Radical Republicans in Congress were offended that elected officials from former Confederate states would resume their positions in the federal government, as if the Civil War had never happened. The lawmakers were hell bent on enforcing a more punitive

Reconstruction plan, whereby a *majority* of Southern voters would have to sign the loyalty oath, instead of a mere ten percent. *Congressional Reconstruction* would also mandate enfranchisement of freedmen and the punishment of ex-Confederate leaders.

Among the most vocal of the Radical Republicans were Representatives Thaddeus Stevens, James Ashley, George W. Julian, and Benjamin Butler, along with Senators Charles Sumner, Benjamin Wade, and Zachariah Chandler. When President Johnson issued his Amnesty Proclamation during the congressional recess, Stevens shared his frustrations in a letter to Sumner: "Is there no way to arrest the insane course of the President in Washington?" Stevens followed up with a letter to President Johnson, recommending a special session of Congress, and warned him that Congress would not stand idly by: "Reconstruction is a delicate question… it is a question for the legislative power exclusively." Unimpressed, Johnson simply ignored Stevens protest.

Several Republican lawmakers returned to the Capitol in late June, hoping to convince the President to call a special session to deal with Reconstruction. Johnson flatly refused to consider their request, and insisted that the Chief Executive was constitutionally empowered to deal with the issues at hand.

Partisan politics also played a role in the widening breech between the President and Congress. Newly elected Representatives and Senators from the South would be Democrats, as there was no established Republican Party south of the Mason-Dixon Line. Those newly-seated lawmakers, appreciative of Johnson's lenient approach to Reconstruction, would be inclined to support him in the 1868 election.

The Republicans were also fearful of losing their congressional majorities with an influx of Southern Democrats. In 1865, the Republicans held majorities in the Senate (39 to 11) and the House of Representatives (140 to 43). If Southerners were allowed to return to Congress before the end of the year, the total number of Democratic lawmakers would increase to as much as 33 in the Senate and 101 in the House.

While universal black suffrage was a cornerstone of the Radical Republican ideal, President Johnson did not believe the federal government had any constitutional right to set voting requirements for individual states. Opposed to wholesale enfranchisement of former slaves, Johnson saw merit in select cases, as evidenced in a telegram that he sent to Mississippi Governor, William Sharkey: "If you could extend the elective franchise to all persons of color who can read the Constitution of the United States in English and write their names, and to all persons of color who own real estate valued at not less that $250.00, and pay taxes thereon, you would completely disarm the adversary, and set an example the other states will follow." Johnson clarified his position during an interview with a New Orleans reporter, advocating voting rights for blacks who could read and understand the Constitution—mirroring a plan previously adopted by the state of Massachusetts: "There are not 500 in Louisiana, who can answer that test, but it will be doing justice to all, and stop this clamor."

While President Johnson offered unsolicited advice to Southern political leaders concerning black suffrage, he made no effort to implement his suggestions, yielding to the sanctity of States' Rights. Johnson believed that black suffrage "was not a natural right, but a political right," pointing out that only five New England states, all with miniscule black populations, had given Negroes the right to vote. Ultimately, none of the former Confederate states would ever *voluntarily* enfranchise a former slave. Alabama's Provisional Governor echoed the sentiments of many white Southerners: "I'll emigrate if Negroes get to vote!"

Johnson argued that universal black suffrage would be disastrous, suggesting freed slaves would simply vote in line with their former masters, ultimately leading to animosity between Negroes and poor whites. At the core of the issue, Johnson simply could not overcome his racism: "I am for a white man's government in America."

Initially, many Republicans, excluding the Radicals, were content to allow the President to implement his plan for Reconstruction.

General Ulysses S. Grant hailed Johnson as "the right man in the right place," and urged his election in 1868.

In the months while Congress was in recess, Presidential Reconstruction established a tenuous foothold. Seaports, federal courts, and post offices reopened across the South. After eight months in office, Johnson appeared to be well on the way to promoting *Restoration* of the former Confederacy; the President believed the term *Restoration* was more palatable than *Reconstruction*.

The Radical Republicans in Congress were not only frustrated by their exclusion from the Reconstruction process, but also deplored Johnson's liberal issuance of pardons. As the year progressed, the President was granting pardons at the rate of 100 per day. Johnson empowered Provisional Governors and presidential clerks to issue pardons, in spite of the fact that many former Rebels were actually committing perjury when affirming the loyalty oath. By the end of 1865, the President had granted over 7000 pardons to former Confederates. In one case, a former Confederated General was issued a pardon 10 days *after* he was elected to statewide office!

Johnson bristled at congressional criticism of his Reconstruction policies, and continued to vigorously exert his executive privileges. Laboring diligently in the White House, the President was up by 6:00 a.m., and read a handful of newspapers before breakfast. He was in the office by 9:00 a.m., and worked until 4:00 p.m. Dinner was served at 5:00 p.m., followed by a walk or carriage ride. From 9:00 to 11:00 p.m., Johnson returned to his office to receive visitors.

Johnson's organizational skills and work ethic were never in question. He employed six full time secretaries (compared to his predecessor's two), and the presidential offices on the second floor executive wing teemed with activity (the ground floor West Wing offices were not utilized until the next century—today, the Lincoln Bedroom occupies the one time location of President Johnson's office). Johnson scheduled Cabinet meetings on Tuesdays and Fridays. During crisis periods, however, the Cabinet met daily, including Sundays.

While his oratorical skills were undeniable, Johnson's writing often contained misspellings and grammatical errors, betraying his lack of formal education. To that end, the President routinely dictated correspondence to his secretaries, complaining that his painful right arm, broken in the 1857 train derailment, made it difficult for him to use pen and paper. Ever sensitive to criticism, Johnson defended his writing skills: "It's a damn poor mind that can only think of one way to spell a word!"

After Mary Todd Lincoln vacated the premises on June 9, 1865, President Johnson officially moved into the White House. Ten days later, his oldest daughter, Martha Peterson (whose husband, David, would soon become a U.S. Senator from Tennessee), and her two children joined him in the presidential mansion. On August 16th, Johnson's wife, Eliza, sons, Robert and Andrew, Jr., and his second daughter, Mary Stover and her three children, joined the rest of the family. For the first time in Johnson's Washington D.C. political career, the entire family lived under the same roof. As a house warming gift of sorts, Congress appropriated $ 125,000.00 to redecorate the White House, which had fallen into a state of disrepair over the years.

Robert Johnson soon created problems for his father. The President's wayward son had been forced to resign his military commission (Colonel) with the 1st Tennessee Union Calvary because of drunkenness. Once in the White House, Robert continued drinking and was accused of bringing prostitutes in the mansion. In May of 1866, the President dispatched his troubled son on a *diplomatic mission* to Africa, South America, China, and Japan, effectively removing him from Washington D.C. for nearly a year. Ever mindful of the taxpayer's money, Johnson paid for Robert's excursion out of his own pocket.

With his strenuous work ethic, Johnson indulged few recreational activities. However, he came to appreciate baseball, which was well on its way to becoming America's past time. On occasion, the President took time to watch pickup games organized on the South Grounds of the White House. He occasionally played checkers, and found circuses and minstrel shows amusing. However, Johnson's preferred method of relaxation was to share a glass of Tennessee bourbon with select friends, talking politics. He did not regularly attend church, but on occasion would accompany the First Lady to Methodist services.

Johnson delighted in the presence of his grandchildren in the White House, often taking them to wade in the shallows of nearby Rock Creek. One observer noted that children were the sole source of Johnson's "rare smiles." During the Johnson Administration, the White House hosted its first *Easter Egg Roll* for the enjoyment of the Capitol City youth; the tradition dated back to the Madison Presidency, but had previously been held on Capitol Hill.

Because of her poor health, the First Lady rarely made public appearances. Johnson's daughter, Martha, most often served as the official hostess during White House social events. Outgoing and courteous, the First Daughter was well liked by the majority of Washington insiders.

The *Provisional* Southern Governors, appointed by President Johnson, eventually called for state conventions, where the 13th Amendment was ratified; the amendment, abolishing slavery, became a national law on December 18, 1865, after ratification by the requisite 3/4 of the states. The former Confederate states also repealed previous Secession Ordinances. After the constitutional conventions, local, state, and federal elections were held throughout the Deep South.

The electoral results in the South were predictable, with conservatives and former Secessionists winning most of the races. In blatant defiance of the 13th Amendment, the newly elected Southern state legislatures soon passed *Black* Codes to regulate the labor and civil rights of former slaves. Under Black Code mandates, freed blacks were forced to sign annual labor contracts and were required to present their work licenses on demand. They were forbidden to practice a skilled trade without a license. If a laborer left his job, he was forced to forfeit an entire year's worth of wages. Rigid apprenticeships were established for younger blacks, who were subjected to corporal punishment if they displeased their employers. In South

Carolina, many former slaves were simply reclassified as *servants*. Strict vagrancy laws allowed white law enforcement officers to arrest idle *freedmen*, who were sentenced to government work details or loaned out to private employers. Freedmen were also prevented from testifying in court, serving on juries, and owning property. They also could not rent land outside of incorporated towns. Blacks were also not allowed to possess firearms or other weapons. The combined effect of Black Codes and disfranchisement established cruel, second-class citizenship for former slaves.

At the end of 1865, four former Confederate Generals, five Colonels, and Alexander Stephens, the former Vice-President of the Confederacy, all of whom had received special pardons from President Johnson, were elected to Congress. The Radical Republicans were appalled, and could not understand Johnson's devotion to States' Rights, unwillingness to condemn the Black Codes, opposition to black suffrage, and leniency toward former Confederate leaders.

On September 12th, President Johnson ordered lands confiscated during the war returned to their Southern owners, displacing freedmen who had been settled on former plantations by the Union Army. In November, Johnson suspended collection of the *cotton tax* to ease the financial burden on Southern planters. Whenever, possible, the President ordered removal of black occupation troops, whose presence infuriated white Southerners. Johnson also allowed Southern militia to organize; many of them took the liberty of forcefully *restoring order* among blacks.

In a newspaper interview on September 11th, Johnson declared: "I am of Southern people, and I love them and will do all in my power to restore them." As Presidential Reconstruction progressed, Johnson appeared to be gaining the support of white Southerners, fueling his hopes of establishing a *great Conservative Party* that would propel his election to the presidency in 1868.

On December 5, 1865, during his annual congressional message, President Johnson boldly declared: "All pretended acts of secession, were, from the beginning, null and void." He stressed the importance of welcoming the Southern states back into the Union, enabling the federal government to resume its normal functions. The President predicted, in due time, every state would eventually grant suffrage to eligible voters, regardless of race.

Johnson was pleased with his efforts to restore the Union; an opinion shared by others. Indiana Governor, Oliver P. Morton, a Moderate Republican, wrote the President: "I can't be mistaken, the great body of the people of the North will endorse your doctrine and policy, and this, the members of Congress will find out before they are ninety days older..."

On December 2nd, two days before Congress convened, Massachusetts Senator, Charles Sumner, an avowed Radical Republican, visited Andrew Johnson in the White House. During their two hour visit, neither man could convince the other to give ground on the management of Reconstruction. Adding insult to injury, at the conclusion of the meeting, when Sumner retrieved his hat from the floor, he discovered that the President had inadvertently used it as a spittoon!

By December of 1865, 10 of the 11 former Confederate states had adopted the mandates of Presidential Reconstruction (Texas would follow in March of 1866). In the eyes of President Johnson, the Union had been *restored*. When the 39th Congress convened on December 4th, newly elected Representatives and Senators from Louisiana, North Carolina, and Maryland were ready to take their seats.

With Radical Republicans, like Stevens, Sumner, and Chandler leading the way, Congress was unwilling to accept the premise that Reconstruction was complete. Moreover, the Radicals were fed up with President Johnson's unilateral declarations.

On December 4, 1865, prodded by its Radical Republican leaders, both houses of Congress ruled Presidential Reconstruction null and void, and established a *Joint Committee of Fifteen* (aka *Joint Commission on Reconstruction*). The legislative committee, consisting of nine Representatives and six Senators, refused to seat their newly elected Southern colleagues: "No member shall be received into either House from any of the said so-called Confederate states."

Congress also refused to pay the expenses of Southern Senators and Representatives, forcing most of them to return home.

Declaring that the Southern states were conquered provinces, Representative Thaddeus Stevens insisted that the newly emancipated slaves required protection from the federal government: "This Congress is bound together for them (the former slaves) until they can take care of themselves."

The Joint Committee of Fifteen took now claimed full authority to judge whether the former Confederate states were eligible for readmission to Congress. After interviewing 145 witnesses regarding the mistreatment of freedmen by the white Southern majority, the committee petitioned President Johnson to take no further action concerning Reconstruction, without the consent of Congress.

The remaining three years of the Johnson Presidency would be dominated by an epic struggle between the executive and legislative branches of the government concerning the direction and constitutionality of Reconstruction.

Chapter 14

I know I am right

Andrew Johnson believed that his plan for Reconstruction would force the former Confederate states to acknowledge their transgressions, without humiliation. He was equally certain that Presidential Reconstruction was consistent with the principles outlined in the United States Constitution. Johnson's interpretation, however, was clouded by personal prejudice: "The white race was (is) superior to the black."

Johnson was not alone in his prejudice, nor was bigotry limited to Southerners. In 1865, voters in Connecticut, Wisconsin, and Minnesota defeated proposals granting black suffrage. Two years later, an amendment granting black suffrage was defeated in Ohio, compelling a state Democratic leader to declare the "thralldom of Niggerism" must be halted. For many Americans, the end of slavery was not synonymous with full equality for blacks. From a political perspective, Johnson thought racial prejudice would unite Northern and Southern Democrats, who would support him in the 1868 presidential election.

On February 7, 1866, a group of freedmen, including renowned civil rights leader, Frederick Douglas, visited the White House to lobby for universal suffrage. Douglas offered an earnest plea: "You have the power to save or destroy us, to bless us or blast us—I mean our whole race." President Johnson advised his visitors that voting rights should be determined by individual states, and government-mandated black suffrage would lead to race wars. At the same time, the President made a half-hearted attempt to reassure Douglas and his cohorts: "I have great faith in the people." Johnson further predicted that Southern states would eventually "do what is right."

Douglas and his companions were disappointed and frustrated after their meeting with Johnson. At the same time, the President was angered by the confrontation with the freedmen, responding with a racist tirade: "Those damned sons of bitches thought they had me in a trap. I know that damned Douglas. He's just like any Nigger, and he would sooner cut a white man's throat than not."

At the beginning of 1866, when congressional Republicans initiated steps to take control of Reconstruction, Andrew Johnson was in a position to forge a compromise with a majority of the lawmakers, thereby reshaping his legacy. His principle opponents were the Radical Republicans, who were hell bent to mandate full equal rights and suffrage for Negroes. While energetic and vocal, the Radicals were a minority faction in Congress. The more numerous Moderate Republicans wanted to keep former Secessionists from returning to power, but had no real inclination to promote black suffrage. The Conservative Republicans (numbering only a dozen or so in both houses of Congress) and the 54 congressional Democrats had no agenda beyond what had already been accomplished—ending slavery and preserving the Union. Unfortunately, Johnson was no collaborator, and by the end of year, would manage to alienate all but a handful of Democratic lawmakers.

Thaddeus Stevens was among the most zealous and vocal of the Radical Republicans. Determined to punish the former Confederate states, Stevens proposed redistribution of the "forfeited estates of the enemy" to provide land holdings for freed slaves. The majority of Stevens' colleagues, both Democratic and Republican, viewed seizure of private property as entirely too radical, and blocked his proposal.

In February of 1866, Congress passed legislation indefinitely extending the life of the *Freedmen's Bureau,* leading to the first major showdown between the legislative and executive branches of government. The bill passed both houses of Congress with near unanimous Republican support. After meeting face-to-face with the President, a handful of Moderate Republican lawmakers mistakenly believed that Johnson had agreed to support extension of the Freedmen's Bureau. Shelby Cullum, a Republican Congressman from Illinois, was among the group who consulted with Johnson, and believed that a compromise had been reached: "A veto at that time was almost unheard of."

Nonetheless, President Johnson vetoed the renewal of the *Freedmen's Bureau Bill*, which would have expanded the governmental agency, and increased its judicial powers to prevent discrimination against former slaves. Officially known as the *Bureau of Refugees, Freedmen, and Abandoned Lands*, the agency had been created in March of 1865, shortly before the assassination of President Lincoln, as a subdivision of the War Department. The Freedmen's Bureau, staffed by some 900 agents spread across the South, was in charge of selling and renting lands confiscated during the Civil War, assisting black communities with the establishment of schools and churches, helping freedmen negotiate fair contract and land sale agreements, and providing family services (such as location of lost relatives and mediation of domestic disputes).

Johnson was fundamentally opposed to the mission of the Freedmen's Bureau, and was particularly unhappy that the military could override the rights of freely elected civilian governments. He also questioned the need for renewal legislation, as the bureau's existing mandate was not slated to expire until 1867. Johnson further asserted that lawmakers did not have the authority to rule on matters involving Southern states that were not yet represented in Congress. Absent congressional representation by all the states, Johnson asserted that the President, "chosen by people of all states," could best provide for national interests, as opposed to lawmakers elected "from a single district." Johnson also believed it was unjust for the government to take land from private owners. From a practical perspective, the President opposed the appropriation of federal funds to support a particular segment of the population, and complained that the Freedmen's Bureau would cost "more than the entire sum expended in any one year (since) the Administration of the second Adams."

On a personal level, Johnson was disinclined to provide black Americans with property or special privileges, believing it would hinder ambition and deemphasize the value of hard work. According to Johnson, special assistance from the Freedmen's Bureau would injure the "character and prospects" of Negroes and promote a "life of indolence." Viewing himself as the prime example of a *self-made man,* the President expected Negroes to climb the economic ladder, without governmental assistance. Bound by racial prejudice, Johnson believed blacks deserved *protection,* but not *equality.* In his racially coded veto message, the President deemed the "immense patronage" extended by the Freedmen's Bureau was unconstitutional. He pointed out, heretofore; Congress had never purchased land, provided economic support, or established schools for "our own people."

When Johnson vetoed the Freedmen's Bill, Frederick Douglas attacked the President during a speech in Chicago: "It is said that Andrew Johnson is following in the footsteps of Abraham Lincoln. It is a foul and black slander on the dead…Jeff Davis was a great traitor, but he was a consistent traitor. He was a wolf, but not a wolf in sheep's clothing…He did not put himself at the head of the Rebel cause to betray it, as Andrew Johnson has done to the loyal cause." In sharp contrast to Douglas' scathing attack, the headlines in a Southern newspaper hailed Johnson: *GREAT VICTORY FOR THE WHITE MAN.*

The Freedmen's Bureau Bill had been proposed by a Moderate Republican, Senator Lyman Trumball of Illinois, and passed both the Senate and House with unanimous Republican support. When President Johnson vetoed the legislation, he found himself opposing *all* Republicans, not just the Radicals.

Playing a risky political game, Johnson chose to alienate Moderate and Conservative Republicans, hoping that Southern whites and Northern Democrats, who were eager to see the Freedmen's Bureau expire, would rally behind him. A North Carolina state legislator explained Johnson's dilemma: "If the President vetoes, then the fuss commences between him and the Radicals; if he signs, all will go on well with them, but raise a fuss in the South."

In addition to vetoing the Freedmen's Bill, Johnson also nullified the *confiscation* and *resale* of Southern lands, eliminating one of the essential functions of the agency, once again asserting that blacks should become self-supporting as a result of their own hard work, rather than benefit from government largess. On October 10, 1865, President Johnson lectured the 1st Regiment of the *D.C. Colored Troops*: "You will soon be mustered out of the ranks. It is for you to establish the great fact that you are fit and qualified to be free. Here, freedom is not a mere idea, but is something that exists in fact. Freedom is not the privilege to live in idleness. Liberty does not mean a resort to low saloons and other places of disreputable character. Freedom and liberty do not mean that people ought to live in licentiousness; but liberty means simply to be industrious, to be virtuous, and to be upright in all dealings and relations with men…"

The Radical Republicans in Congress were enraged by Johnson's obstructionist tactics. While the House of Representatives overrode the President's veto of the Freedmen's Bureau Bill,109 to 40, the Senate fell 2 votes short of the necessary 2/3rd majority (in the end, 5 Moderate Republican Senators joined their Democratic colleagues in voting to sustain the veto). An angry and vengeful Radical Republican, Senator Benjamin Wade, introduced an unsuccessful resolution to limit all future Presidents to a single term in office. Many Moderate Republicans saw the handwriting on the wall, including Maine Senator, William Pitt Fessenden, who predicted that the President "will and must veto every other bill we pass."

Outside of Congress, the President's veto was scrutinized by the press. *Harper's Weekly* challenged Johnson's support of the racist status quo in the former Confederacy: "If the President believes that the word of the nation sacredly pledged to freedmen will be kept by the Black Codes of South Carolina and Mississippi, his faith would move mountains."

With characteristic bellicosity, Johnson personalized his conflict with Congress during a Washington's Birthday address. On February 22, 1866, against the advice of his aides, who were worried that he would lash out at the congressional Republicans, the President spoke to a gathering of citizens on the White House grounds: "I stand for the country, and though my enemies may traduce, slander, and vituperate, I must say that has no force." Johnson further extended the "right hand of fellowship" to the South, and also attacked Representative Thaddeus Stevens and Senator Charles Sumner by name. The President accused Radical Republicans of "being opposed to and looking to destroy the fundamental principles of government."

The Republicans were understandably offended by Johnson's remarks and quickly circulated rumors that the President had been drunk during his Washington's Birthday speech. During his self-serving, hour-long speech, Johnson referred to himself more than 200 times, and provided Radical Republican lawmakers with ample political fodder. Acid-tongued Thaddeus Stevens referred to Johnson as "His Accidency." Worse yet, Conservative Northerners, who were already concerned about the President's vindictiveness, now questioned his judgment.

A second showdown between the executive and legislative branches occurred after Congress passed the *Civil Rights Act* in March of 1866. The new legislation granted citizenship to all persons born in the United States (except American Indians) "regardless of race, color, or previous condition (servitude)."

Republican Senator, John Sherman of Ohio, was primed for Johnson's reaction: "If the President vetoes the Civil Rights Bill, I believe we shall be obligated to draw our swords for a fight and throw away our scabbards." As anticipated, Johnson vetoed the legislation, arguing that it was wrong to grant instant citizenship to freed blacks, while forcing foreigners to go through a five-year naturalization process. He proclaimed the Civil Rights Bill as unconstitutional: "It is another step, or rather stride, toward centralization of all legislative powers in the national government." Johnson predicted the Civil Rights Act would "resuscitate the spirit of rebellion" by creating race wars: "The distinction of race and color is by the bill made to appear in favor of colored and against the white race."

In April of 1866, after months of frustration, with a single vote majority, the Republicans were finally able to claim victory by overriding the President's veto of the Civil Rights Act, marking the first time in history that Congress had overridden the veto of a major piece of legislation. Radicals and Moderates alike, joined forces to defeat Johnson, with only 4 Senate Republicans voting to sustain the veto. Johnson angrily declared that the Republicans were as disruptive as the Secessionists, because the latter favored "destroying the government to preserve slavery," while the former wanted to "break up the government to protect slavery." Johnson voiced little doubt concerning the justness of his veto: "I know I am right, and I am damned if I do not adhere." The *New York Herald* described the growing conflict in Washington D.C.: "The veto of the Freedmen's Bureau Bill was but the distant thunder announcing the approaching storm. The veto of the Civil Rights Act was the storm itself."

After vetoing the Civil Rights Bill, Johnson lost his final chance to collaborate with Moderate Republican lawmakers. Most Moderates now believed that the President was determined to "wreck the Republican Party." Many historians consider this veto as the single biggest mistake of Johnson's presidency.

In its April 14, 1886 edition, *Harper's Weekly* ridiculed Johnson's veto message: "Having freed a man from chattel slavery, is the Government bound to look on passively and see him reduced to virtual slavery, by a state vagrant law, for a trivial offense? The President, indeed, asks in his veto whether the present laws are not sufficient to protect the rights of freedmen. What rights? If they are neither citizens, nor domiciled aliens, nor foreigners, what rights have they?" A week later, a *Harper's* editorialist wrote: "If man cannot own property and exercise every right that springs from its possession, he is not free."

Like the legislation extending the Freedmen's Bureau, the Civil Rights Bill had been a Moderate Republican proposal, and Johnson's veto was a slap in the face to non-Radical lawmakers. Many Moderate Republican Representatives and Senators had difficulty understanding why Johnson opposed the measure, since it contained no provision for black suffrage. With his second veto, the President irrevocably damaged his relationship with the faction of Republicans who might have saved his presidency.

While advocating lenient Reconstruction, President Johnson's anger toward the imprisoned Jefferson Davis was much slower to melt. On April 25, 1866, Varina Davis, who had not seen her husband in nearly a year, wrote Johnson an impassioned letter: "I hear my husband is failing rapidly. Can I come to him? Can you refuse me? Answer."

After conferring with Secretary of War Stanton, Johnson allowed Varina to visit her husband. Within days of her initial visit, she was allowed to move into Fortress Monroe and live with him.

Congress gained a measure of revenge against President Johnson when he nominated his legal aide, Henry Stanbery, for a vacant position on the United States Supreme Court. Stanbery had assisted Johnson in drafting his veto of the Civil Rights Act, and spiteful Radical Republican lawmakers spearheaded a vote to eliminate the Supreme Court vacancy, reducing the number of justices to eight, and thwarted Stanberry's opportunity to join the high court.

On the heels of their twin victories against President Johnson, Congress passed the 14th Amendment in June of 1866, which modified Article I, Section 2 of the United States Constitution. The new amendment consisted of 3 sections. The 1st part mandated that "no state shall make or enforce any law which shall abridge the privileges or immunities of the United States; nor shall any state deprive any person of life, liberty, or property, without due process of law; nor deny to any person within its jurisdiction the equal protection of the laws." Section 2 eliminated the 3/5th rule that had existed prior to the abolition of slavery (by now counting freed blacks as full voters, Southern states would actually *gain* 12 Congressional seats). The controversial 3rd section prohibited former Confederate civilian and military leaders from serving in federal office until a *2/3rd* majority of each house of Congress had removed the disability. After passing both houses of Congress, the proposed 14th Amendment was passed to the states, with a promise that all former members of the Confederacy would be readmitted to the Union upon its ratification.

Now engaged in a full-scale confrontation with congressional Republicans, Johnson encouraged the Southern states to remain defiant, declaring that the 14th Amendment was unconstitutional, because it was inappropriate to amend the Constitution without congressional representation from *all* states. Ultimately, 10 of the 11 former Confederate states refused to ratify the amendment, which proved inconsequential, when a sufficient number of states outside the Deep South ratified the measure. The new amendment was officially enacted into law on July 9, 1868. Johnson had, yet again, opposed a Moderate Republican proposal that had nothing to do with black suffrage. When Southern states failed to ratify the 14th Amendment, Congress once again refused to seat their elected Senators and Congressmen.

In July, Congress passed another *Freedmen's Bureau Bill*, which President Johnson promptly vetoed. Not surprisingly, the veto was overridden. Only 3 Republican Senators, including the Conservatives, voted to sustain Johnson's veto.

In the summer of 1866, racial violence erupted in the Deep South. During the month of May, white law enforcement officers in Memphis killed 46 black citizens during several days of rioting (2 whites also died). In July, a white mob in New Orleans attacked an assembly promoting black suffrage. In the resulting melee, 47 people were killed, and 140 were wounded—the casualty count included both blacks and whites. The racial violence in Tennessee and Louisiana contradicted President Johnson's claim that Southern states were peacefully reorganizing under the auspices of Presidential Reconstruction.

Many Northerners held President Johnson directly responsible for the violence in the Deep South. *Harper's Weekly* condemned the riots in New Orleans: "It was a preconceived massacre of white and colored Union men by late Rebel soldiers, with the assistance of the mob and the police, under the general direction of Mayor Monroe, who, while an unpardoned Rebel, was elected to office, and was pardoned by President Johnson expressly that he might assume it. The facts of the case are appalling."

White Southerners, 9,000,000 in number, were determined to limit the power and influence of the 4,000,000 freedmen, utilizing whatever means necessary. A familiar refrain echoed throughout the Deep South: "If we let a Nigger get equal with us, the next thing we know, he'll be ahead of us." White intimidation and racially motivated violence became a tragic way of life in the former Confederacy. Vigilante groups like the *Knights of the Golden Circle*, the *Teutonic Knights*, and the *Ku Klux Klan* were organized to deal with the so-called *Nigger problem*. By the end of 1865, angry white citizens in South Carolina, North Carolina, Mississippi, Georgia, and Tennessee had attacked 200 former slaves; killing 44 of them; these numbers, however, reflect only the *reported* cases of violence.

On June 25, 1866, Andrew Johnson proposed a convention to establish a new *Union Party*, hoping to counter the growing influence of the Radical Republicans. Johnson envisioned a coalition of Conservative Republicans and Northern Democrats who favored his Reconstruction policies and were motivated to unseat Radical and Moderate lawmakers in the fall congressional elections.

On August 14th, 7000 delegates gathered in Philadelphia for the opening of the Union Party convention. Democrat delegates immediately dominated the proceedings and were unable to forge an alliance with Conservative Republicans, many of whom quit the convention. Johnson's hopes of establishing a viable Conservative Party died before its birth.

The battle between Andrew Johnson and congressional Republicans grew more contentious during the late summer of 1866. The midterm congressional elections promised to be the first test of nationwide support for the President's policies. Under the guise of traveling to Chicago to dedicate a monument to the late Stephen Douglas, a man Johnson had actually despised, the President planned to campaign on behalf of Conservatives, and to convince Northern voters that Presidential Reconstruction was in the best interest of the entire country. Johnson ignored the counsel of many of his friends and advisers, including Secretary of Navy, Gideon Welles, who deemed such a trip as undignified for a President. On August 27th, Johnson departed Washington D.C. for what would become known as the infamous three-week, *Swing around the Circle* campaign tour.

Secretary of State, William Seward, once described Andrew Johnson as "the best stump speaker in the country," and the President hoped his oratorical gifts would convince the American people to support Presidential Reconstruction. A distinguished group, including Seward, General Ulysses S. Grant, Admiral David Farragut, and Secretary of the Navy, Gideon Welles, joined Johnson on his circuitous tour of the Northeast and Midwest.

With bombastic flair, Johnson addressed crowds along the way, dramatizing his own rise from humble tailor to President of the United States. Incredibly, he likened himself to Jesus Christ, who was generously pardoning the "repentant sinners" from the South. Johnson also assailed Radical Republicans for trying to keep the Union from reuniting, likening opposition party leaders to a "subsidized gang of hirelings and traducers."

In Springfield, Illinois, Johnson visited Abraham Lincoln's grave, much to the chagrin of the former First Lady. Mary Todd Lincoln, who was unwilling to mask her dislike of Johnson, castigated the current President for "desecrating" her husband's burial site. Mrs. Lincoln loudly denounced Johnson: "The President encountered much that would humiliate any, other than himself, possessing such inordinate vanity and presumption as he does." An editorial in the *Chicago Tribune* amplified the former First Lady's attack on Johnson: "...The country feels that the malice of its sainted dead have been desecrated by the presence of an unworthy successor of its murdered President, whose heart is filled with envy for his greatness and with bitterness for his friends..."

Johnson lashed out at his critics, foolishly declaring that Abraham Lincoln was "lucky" to be dead, or "the vials of wrath would have been poured on him." Undeterred by criticism, Johnson continued to plead his case to voters along the way. In St. Louis, he advocated immediate reconciliation with the former Confederate states: "The bleeding arteries should be tied up." Johnson accused the Radical Republicans of trying to enfranchise the "colored population" at the expense of "white men."

When heckled by the crowds, Johnson's rhetoric grew more outrageous, and he readily assumed the role of martyr: "I have been traduced, I have been slandered, I have been maligned, and I have been called Judas Iscariot." Johnson's continued use of religious metaphors supplied his enemies with abundant ammunition for counter-attacks. The *Chicago Tribune* described the President's St. Louis speech as the "crowning disgrace of a disreputable series." Johnson only added fuel to the fire, when he proclaimed: "I care not for dignity." Rumors immediately circulated that Johnson had been drunk while delivering his intemperate speeches.

A disgusted Ulysses S. Grant wrote his wife during the campaign swing with the President: "I have never been so tired of anything before, as I have been the political stump speeches of Mr. Johnson. I look upon them as a national disgrace." As the tension mounted, Grant went on an alcoholic binge, a not unusual pattern for him during times of stress. In Cleveland, the Civil War hero was so drunk that he was taken off the train for a sobering up cruise across Lake Erie, before rejoining the presidential party in Detroit. By the time the train reached Cincinnati, Grant was fed up and left for good, unwilling to "accompany a man who was deliberately digging his own grave."

The campaign tour rapidly deteriorated, when angry crowds in Indianapolis and Pittsburgh shouted down the President. In Ohio, the Governor and other state officials refused to meet with Johnson. By the time he returned to Washington on September 15th, Johnson's politically-motivated tour had generated considerable controversy, and weakened support for Presidential Reconstruction. Johnson had misjudged the mood of voters, failing to comprehend the near universal fear among Northerners that white Southerners were not only unrepentant for their role in instigating the Civil War, but also were determined to deprive freedmen of their basic rights.

The mainstream press grew increasingly critical of the President. The *New York Independent* published a scathing review of Johnson's campaign excursion: "For the first time in the history of our country, the people have been witness to the mortifying spectacle of the President going about, from town to town, accompanied by the prominent members of the Cabinet, on an electioneering raid, denouncing his opponents, bandying epithets with men in the crowd, and praising himself and his policies. Such a humiliating exhibition has never been seen, nor anything even approaching it." A political pundit predicted the Swing around the Circle tour would cost the Democrats 1,000,000 Northern votes.

While a few men, like Secretary of State, William Seward, and Secretary of the Navy, Gideon Welles remained loyal to President Johnson, other members of the Administration turned against him. Isaac Arnold, a U.S. Postal Department official and close friend of Abraham Lincoln, tendered an angry letter of resignation to the President: "You have betrayed the great Union Party which elected Abraham Lincoln...How can you, Mister President, occupy the Executive Mansion as successor to Lincoln?" Arnold's missive recommended the "overthrow" of Johnson's policies: "I retire from office that I may more freely and effectively aid in that overthrow." Former Vice-President, Hannibal Hamlin, joined the dissenters, when he resigned his position as the Ports Collector of Boston. By August of 1866, three Cabinet officers, Attorney General, James Speed, Secretary of the Interior, James Harlan, and Postmaster General, William Dennison, had tendered letters of resignation.

As 1866 drew to a close, Andrew Johnson's grasp on power grew more tenuous. The President's veto of a bill granting suffrage to blacks living in Washington D.C. was overridden by Congress—the third such occurrence in less than a year. On Election Day, Republicans swept to victory in the Northeast and Midwest, widening their majorities in both the House (173 to 53) and Senate (43 to 9).

Ohio Senator and future President, James A. Garfield, relished the prospect of a Republican-controlled Congress directing Reconstruction. Garfield was certain the former Confederate states "would not cooperate with us in rebuilding what they destroyed," and boldly predicted that Congressional Reconstruction would "remove rubbish and build from the bottom."

With veto-proof majorities in both houses of Congress, Johnson had no chance of derailing the Republican agenda. In December of 1866, during his annual congressional address, the President once again asked lawmakers to admit Congressmen and Senators from the Deep South, who had been elected under the terms of Presidential Reconstruction. As expected, Congress ignored Johnson's recommendations. By the end of 1866, Presidential Reconstruction was dead, and, in the coming year, the Republicans would implement even harsher policies.

Andrew Johnson began 1867 by vetoing legislation establishing statehood for Nebraska and Colorado. Congress sustained the Colorado veto, as many lawmakers agreed that the territory's population (only 30,000) was too small to warrant statehood. The Nebraska veto, however, was overridden, and the Senate quickly gained 2 additional Republican Senators. Nebraska's admission to the Union marked the only time in history that statehood was granted over a presidential veto.

On January 3, 1867, Representative Thaddeus Stevens introduced the *First Reconstruction Act,* legislation deemed necessary "to protect those people (freedmen) from the barbarians who are now daily murdering them." A month later, after committee amendments, the renamed *Military Reconstruction Act* passed both houses of Congress.

President Johnson believed the new law violated the rights of Southern whites in order to "protect Niggers." He angrily informed his secretary that before he signed such legislation, "I would sever my right arm from my body." On March 2nd, the President sent his veto message to Capitol Hill. That same day, Congress overrode President Johnson' veto of the Military Reconstruction Act, which replaced the provisional Southern governments established during the early months of Johnson's Presidential Reconstruction; Tennessee, having already regained admission to the Union, was the lone exception. In their place, Congress established 5 *military districts,* encompassing the 10 remaining states of the former Confederacy. *Military District Commanders* were granted the power to enforce laws and oversee elections, as well as override the authority of state and local governments, including the replacement of previously elected officials. The new legislation also required the former Con-

federate States to ratify the 14ᵗʰ Amendment and draft new constitutions, guaranteeing black suffrage.

Under the watchful eye of military rule, blacks were allowed
to vote, run for office, and serve on juries. Across the Deep South,
some 700,000 African Americans registered to vote. In Louisiana,
Mississippi, Alabama, Florida, and South Carolina, black voters soon
outnumbered their white counterparts. Government-enforced
desegregation and universal suffrage led to cries of hypocrisy from
angry Southerners, who were quick to point out that only 5 northern
states allowed their black citizens to vote.

For the next ten years, Congressional Reconstruction would be
forced upon bitter white Southerners, fostering regional bitterness.
An epic battle between States' Rights and the power and might of
the Federal Government would occupy center stage in the century
to follow.

Congressional Republicans were now in complete charge of
Reconstruction, but Andrew Johnson, with two years remaining in
his presidential term, remained a thorn in the side of reform-minded
lawmakers. Accordingly, many Republican lawmakers were eager
to dispose of Johnson prior to the conclusion of his presidency.
With passage of the *Tenure of Office Act*, Johnson's opponents de-
vised the perfect bait to lure and entrap the stubborn and impulsive
President.

Chapter 15

The Rubicon is crossed

While Andrew Johnson had never fully trusted Edwin Stanton, he had encouraged the Secretary of War to remain in office, along with the entirety of Lincoln's Cabinet, hoping to maintain continuity after his predecessor's assassination. Stanton had been given significant power during the Lincoln Administration, and to his credit, had performed admirably during the Civil War. In the early hours after President Lincoln was shot, it had been Stanton, instead of Vice-President Johnson, who assumed the leadership role.

The fifty-three year-old Stanton, a native of Ohio, was a successful attorney, who gave up a lucrative law practice to enter public service, serving as President James Buchanan's Attorney General prior to Lincoln's election to the presidency. Bespectacled, with a stern countenance and intimidating glare, Stanton was blunt and outspoken, once likening Abraham Lincoln to an ape, when the two young attorneys were involved in litigating a patent case. Lincoln apparently did not hold a grudge, and named Stanton Secretary of War in 1862, replacing an ineffectual and corrupt Simon Cameron.

Stanton eventually became Lincoln's closest adviser, as the two dealt with the endless daily challenges of the Civil War. It was Stanton who took charge of the apprehension, prosecution, and punishment of the individuals responsible for Lincoln's assassination. With the ascension of Andrew Johnson to the presidency, Stanton believed the inexperienced Tennessean would heed his advice and counsel concerning major policy decisions.

Johnson, however, did not consider Stanton a worthy political mentor. The President was aware that the Secretary of War regularly confided in the Radical Republicans, often sharing information discussed during Cabinet meetings and other private discussions. As Johnson grew angered and dismayed by Stanton's disloyalty, the Secretary of War became equally disillusioned with the President's lenient Reconstruction policies.

When lawmakers passed the *Tenure of Office Act* on March 2, 1867, the Radical Republicans were certain Edwin Stanton would be an irresistible target for the impetuous President. The Tenure of Office Act prohibited presidential removal of any government official who had been appointed with the *advice* and *consent* of the Senate, until a majority of the Senators confirmed a replacement. If Congress was in recess, the President could *suspend* the government official and appoint an *Ad Interim* replacement. However, once Congress reconvened, the President would have to explain his rational for suspension of the appointed official. The removal of the appointee would become permanent, only if a *majority* of Senators *concurred* with the President's decision. If the Senate refused to *affirm* the suspension, the officer would be allowed to resume his governmental post.

Not surprisingly, President Johnson vetoed the Tenure of Office Act, asserting that the legislation was unconstitutional, and proclaimed the powers of appointment and dismissal of government officials, particularly Cabinet officers, were the prerogative of the Commander-in-Chief. Congress immediately overrode President Johnson's veto, and the bill was enacted into law. Representative Thaddeus Stevens asserted the essence of congressional privilege: "Though the President is Commander-in-Chief, God willing, he shall obey. He and his minions shall learn that this is not a government of kings and satraps, but a government of the people, and that Congress is the people."

Later that same month, Congress passed the *Second Military Reconstruction Act,* which enabled military personnel to register both black and white voters in the ten Southern states, and to prevent white political leaders from delaying constitutional conventions.

On March 23rd, Johnson vetoed the legislation, which was overridden that same day. Adding insult to injury, Congress passed a rider to the *Appropriations Bill,* mandating that all presidential orders to the military were to be passed through the General of the Army, Ulysses S. Grant.

In the spring of 1867, as President Johnson battled the Republican Congress, Jefferson Davis had been imprisoned for two years and deprived of due process. As vengeful passions slowly subsided, questions arose about the ultimate disposition of the former Confederate President. To the disappointment of many Northerners, Davis was never tried for treason.

Davis' Southern supporters, accompanied by a number of Conservative Northerners, complained that he was being deprived of his constitutional rights. On May 10, 1867, Davis was released from Fortress Monroe. After traveling to the federal courthouse in Richmond, the former prisoner posted bail and was a free man.

On July 13th, Congress passed the *Third Military Reconstruction Act,* whereby military district commanders were empowered to *remove* and *appoint* state officials. The legislation decreed that commanders did not have to abide by "any opinion of any civil officer of the United States" in the unreconstructed states, making civilian governments subordinate to military commanders. Six days later, Johnson delivered his veto to Congress, which was promptly overridden that same day.

In calculating fashion, President Johnson bided his time until Congress adjourned in August of 1867, before promptly suspending Secretary of War Stanton and challenging the new Tenure of Office Act. The President had accumulated a list of grievances against Stanton justifying his suspension—the Secretary of War had failed to support the Administration concerning Presidential Reconstruction, he had demonstrated disloyalty by sharing confidential Cabinet room discussions with members of the Republican Congress, he had criticized the purchase of Alaska (after voting in favor of the acquisition during a Cabinet meeting), and he had allegedly failed to inform the President about specific pages in John Wilkes Booth's diary, which suggested that Mary Suratt's role in the plot to assassinate President Lincoln was based on circumstantial evidence; perhaps insufficient to warrant her execution.

President Johnson was particularly angered by Stanton's duplicity concerning the Tenure of Office Act. During a Cabinet meeting when the proposed law was debated, the Secretary of War had offered his terse opinion: "Any man who would retain his seat in the Cabinet as an adviser, when his advice is not wanted, is not fit for the place, and should resign." Accepting Stanton's statement at face value, Johnson assumed the Secretary of War would resign, if the Commander-in-Chief deemed it necessary.

The President was aware that the Tenure of Office Act allowed him to legally suspend the Secretary of War during a congressional recess. On August 1, 1867, just ten days after Congress adjourned, Johnson informed General Ulysses S. Grant of his plans to suspend Stanton and appoint him as *Ad Interim* Secretary of War. The forty-five year-old Grant, who Johnson had previously promoted to the unprecedented rank of Major General of the United States Army, was hesitant to accept the position. The General's own political ambitions were such that he did not want to offend Republican leaders, as Grant was considered the frontrunner for the GOP presidential nomination in 1868. With trepidation, Grant acquiesced to the President's personal request.

On August 5th, President Johnson sent Edwin Stanton a letter: "Sir: Public consideration of a high character constrains me to say, that your resignation as Secretary of War will be accepted." A day later, a defiant Stanton, bolstered by support from congressional Republicans, answered Johnson's letter: "In reply, I have the honor to state that public considerations of a high character, which alone have induced me to continue at the head of this department, constrain me not to resign the office of Secretary of War, before the next meeting of Congress."

Johnson quietly sought assurance from Grant that he would strictly follow Johnson's orders, if he was appointed Secretary of War. Grant indicated he would serve, but pointed out that his personal support of the 14th Amendment and overall philosophy concerning Reconstruction were at odds with the Johnson Administration. Grant's lukewarm acceptance was satisfactory to Johnson; a decision the President would later regret.

On August 12th, President Johnson composed another letter to Stanton: "By virtue of the power and authority vested in me, as President, by the Constitution and laws of the United States, you are hereby *suspended* from the office of Secretary of War, and will cease to exercise any and all functions pertaining to the same. You will, at once, transfer to General U.S. Grant, who has this day been authorized and empowered to act as Secretary of War *Ad Interim*, all records, books, papers, and other public property in your custody and charge."

That same day, Stanton sent a message to the President via Inspector General, Edmund Schriver, reiterating his opinion that Johnson did not have the authority to suspend him without the consent of the Senate. Out of respect for General Grant, Stanton agreed to *temporarily yield* the office of Secretary of War. Stanton also sent Johnson a stern warning: "The turning point has come— the Rubicon is crossed."

Chapter 16

If so, let it be

On August 17, 1867, five days after suspending Secretary of War Stanton, President Johnson removed General Phillip Sheridan from Command of the Military District encompassing Louisiana and Texas, on grounds that the district commander had interfered with the administration of state governmental affairs. A short time later, Johnson dismissed General Dan Sickles as Military Commander of South and North Carolina. Interim Secretary of War Grant was unhappy with Johnson's dismissal of Sheridan and Sickles, both of whom had been loyal Union Army officers during the Civil War. In short order, Grant began resisting implementation of the President's directives.

Sensing Grant's unhappiness and growing disloyalty, Johnson summoned another Civil War hero, General William T. Sherman, and asked the fiery, red-headed Ohioan to serve as Secretary of War. Sherman quickly declined the offer, citing loyalty to his former commanding officer: "I cannot place myself in a position, even partially antagonistic to Grant." Undeterred, Johnson continued to seek a loyal replacement for Grant.

Johnson further inflamed the Radical Republicans, when he dismissed General John Pope, Military Commander of the district consisting of Alabama, Florida, and Georgia, and General Edward Ord, who commanded the Arkansas and Mississippi districts. In only six months, the President had reassigned four of the six District Commanders put in place by the mandates of Congressional Reconstruction. Johnson justified his actions, alleging that the dismissed military officers had treated citizens of the Deep South in a punitive manner.

On September 9th, Johnson agitated Republican lawmakers, yet again, by issuing a *Second Amnesty Proclamation*. The revised proclamation narrowed the ineligibility criteria to only 3 categories of former Rebels, and lowered the total number of unpardoned Southerners to around 300. By the fall of 1867, the President had issued 13,500 pardons, restoring the civil rights of former Confederates, granting them immunity from prosecution for treason, and prohibiting government confiscation of their property.

In November of 1867, as the controversy over the Tenure of Office Act gathered steam, voters in Minnesota, New Jersey, and Kansas defeated black suffrage proposals. Johnson was quick to point out the hypocritical double standard imposed on Southern states by congressional Republicans.

When Congress reconvened in late 1867, the Radical Republicans were primed to punish Andrew Johnson for his suspension of Stanton. On November 11th, the House Judiciary Committee voted, five to four, to impeach President Johnson for high crimes and misdemeanors, related to his violation of the Tenure of Office Act. Upon learning of the committee's vote, Johnson showed no trepidation: "If so, let it be."

On Capitol Hill, cooler heads soon prevailed, as many lawmakers did not believe the President had violated the Tenure of Office Act by merely *suspending* Stanton. On December 7, 1867, by a vote of 108 to 57, the House of Representatives rejected the resolution of impeachment.

Under the provisions of the Tenure of Office Act, the President was required to inform the Senate of his reasons for suspending an appointed official within *twenty days* of Congress reconvening. Contending the law was unconstitutional, Johnson and his Attorney General, Henry Stanbery, explained to Congress that Edwin Stanton, himself, condemned the Tenure of Office Act at the time of its conception. The President also cited a litany of complaints against the Secretary of War, justifying his suspension and permanent replacement.

Not surprisingly, Republican Senators disagreed with President Johnson's reasoning. On January 13, 1868, lawmakers voted to *not concur* with the suspension, and authorized Stanton to reclaim his position as head of the War Department. Much to the dismay of President Johnson, General Grant immediately relinquished his office to Stanton. Fearing a face-to-face confrontation with Johnson, Grant sent his aide, General Cyrus B. Comstock, to inform the President of his decision.

Johnson was stung by Grant's acquiescence to the Senate ruling, having mistakenly assumed the General would resign the office of Secretary of War, if he could no longer remain loyal to the Administration, and would allow the President sufficient time to appoint a replacement. Grant was summoned to the White House, where he nervously explained that he was fearful of the $10,000.00 fine and 5-year imprisonment if convicted of violating the Tenure of Office Act. Even after Johnson offered to pay any fine levied against Grant and/or personally serve his prison sentence, the General still refused to remain in office.

Though disheartened by Grant's disloyalty, Johnson was determined to confront his political enemies. On February 21st, the President sent Adjutant General, George H. Thomas, to the Secretary of War's office with a letter notifying Stanton that he had been *fired*, and would be replaced by General Lorenzo Thomas. Thomas became Johnson's alternate choice, after General Sherman turned down the offer to serve as Secretary of War.

"Do you wish me to vacate at once, or am I permitted to stay long enough to remove my property?" Stanton asked the Adjutant General.

"Certainly—act at your pleasure," Thomas calmly replied.

After rereading the letter, Stanton grew defiant: "I don't know where I shall obey your orders, or resist them."

A number of congressional Republicans, along with General Grant, urged Stanton to remain in his office. Senator Charles Sumner, among the most ardent of the Radicals, sent Stanton a one-word telegram: *STICK*. Almost immediately, the Senate passed a resolution declaring that the President had no legal authority to dismiss Stanton. Bolstered by his allies in Congress, an angry Stanton ordered General Grant to arrest Lorenzo Thomas, but the politically-minded Grant declined to take action.

As Stanton's designated replacement, Thomas complicated the tense situation by bragging, that if necessary, he would take the office by force. After he threatened to break down the Secretary of War's office door, Stanton asked the Chief Justice of the Supreme Court of the District of Columbia to issue an arrest warrant, charging Thomas with a violation of the Tenure of Office Act.

On the morning of February 22nd, General Thomas was arrested at his home. After posting a $5,000.00 bond, Thomas rushed to the War Department and confronted Stanton. The two men engaged in a heated argument about who was the legitimate Secretary of War. When Stanton ordered Thomas to return to his old office, the aging General refused to budge. Eventually, Thomas grew weary of the argument, complaining about the early morning confrontation: "The next time you have me arrested, don't do it before I get something to eat."

Realizing his subordinate had been placed in a difficult position, Stanton comforted the older man, placing his hand on the General's shoulder and suggesting they share a glass of whiskey. With tempers cooled, a physical confrontation was forestalled. More importantly, Stanton had refused to yield the office.

Later that same month, Stanton dropped the charges against Thomas. The Secretary of War's about face was designed to prevent Thomas from appealing to the U.S. Supreme Court, which might ultimately rule in favor of President Johnson, before the Radical Republicans could exact their revenge.

The showdown between Johnson and the Republican-controlled Congress had reached the point of no return. On Monday, February 24, 1868, just 3 days after Stanton's dismissal, the House of Representatives passed a resolution of impeachment against the President. Introduced by Republican Representative, John Covode of Pennsylvania, the resolution read: "Andrew Johnson, President of the United States, be impeached for *high crimes and misdemeanors* in office." The impeachment resolution passed on a strict party line vote (126 to 47). Representative Thaddeus Stevens angrily defended the rationale for impeachment: "If you don't kill the beast, it will kill you."

Lawmakers based their historical decision on Article II, Section 4 of the United States Constitution, which read: "The President, Vice–President, and all civil officers of the United States shall be removed from office on impeachment for, any conviction of treason, bribery, or high crimes and misdemeanors." Prior to 1868, the House of Representatives had leveled impeachment charges on only 4 occasions. Each of those cases had involved federal judges, and resulted in 2 convictions and 2 acquittals. The President of the United States, however, had never been subjected to impeachment.

In addition to Johnson's violation of the Tenure of Office Act, Congressional Republicans sought to punish him for removing the district military commanders (Sheridan, Sickles, Ord, and Pope), who had been empowered by the mandates of Congressional Reconstruction. Ultimately, *11* articles of impeachment were directed against Andrew Johnson. The first 9 charges were related to violations of the Tenure of Office Act. Article 10 accused Johnson of making speeches against Congress that sowed seeds of *disrespect* and *discontent* among the American people. The 11th charge, referred to as the *Omnibus Article*, accused the President of "intemperate, inflammatory, and scandalous harangues," and was essentially a summary of the first 10 allegations, designed to counteract any legal loophole discovered by Johnson's defense team. Representative Benjamin Butler echoed the harsh sentiments of his fellow Radical Republicans: "By murder, most foul, he (Andrew Johnson) succeeded to the presidency, and is the elect of an assassin to that high office, and not the people!"

After learning of the impeachment vote, Johnson's secretary recalled that the President accepted the news "very coolly and was not at all excited." Seemingly unperturbed, Johnson informed his aides: "If I cannot be President in fact, I will not be President in name alone."

Contrary to popular misconception, impeachment did not equate to conviction. Once the House of Representatives levied formal charges against the President, it would be left up to the Senate to decide his guilt or innocence. The spring of 1868 would be dominated by the historic impeachment trial of Andrew Johnson.

Chapter 17

The American Senate is as corrupt at the Roman Senate

Andrew Johnson's impeachment trial was held in the Senate chambers, with the Chief Justice of the Supreme Court, Salmon P. Chase, presiding. On March 5, 1868, 45 Republican and 9 Democratic Senators were sworn in as jurors. As specified in the United States Constitution, a *2/3rd* majority was necessary to convict the President, and each of the 11 articles would have to be voted on *separately*. The start date for the trial was set for the end of the month.

Seven members of the House of Representatives, collectively known as the *Board of Managers*, were chosen to serve as prosecutors. The prosecution team consisted of 5 Radical Republicans (Thaddeus Stevens of Pennsylvania, George Boutwell and Benjamin Butler of Massachusetts, John Logan of Illinois, and Thomas Williams of Connecticut), and 2 moderates (John Bingham of Ohio and James Wilson of Iowa).

Not surprisingly, Thaddeus Stevens emerged as the most sharp-tongued and vindictive member of the Board of Managers. The seventy-six year-old, clubfooted Pennsylvania native, who wore a wig to cover his typhoid fever-induced baldness, was not unlike his archenemy, Andrew Johnson. Having risen from an undistinguished background, Stevens was often referred to as *The Commoner*. A lifelong bachelor, Stevens was reputed to have had an intimate relationship with his black housekeeper; the scandalous rumor only added to his reputation as a radical. An ardent Abolitionist, the Pennsylvania Congressman was sarcastic and intimidating, and a vocal proponent of harsh Reconstruction. Prior to the abolition of slavery, Stevens' Pennsylvania home had served as a stopping point for runaway slaves seeking freedom via the *Underground Railroad*. Stevens was determined to punish the South for the dual sins of slavery and secession, as evidenced by his inflammatory rhetoric: "Do they not deserve humiliation? If they do not, who does? What criminal, what felon deserves it more?"

Thaddeus Stevens detested Andrew Johnson, and repeatedly slandered the President, labeling him as "The First Great Political Malefactor, The Accidental President, The Practical Demagogue, and The Great Criminal." By 1868, Stevens was the powerful Chairman of the House Ways and Means Committee, reinforcing his vitriol with genuine political power. Stevens boasted that Johnson's impeachment conviction would be easy: "Why, I'll take the man's record, his speeches, and his acts before any impartial jury you can get together, and I'll make them pronounce him either a knave or a fool, without least the trouble."

Stevens was also terminally ill, relying upon two black servants to carry him in and out of the Senate chambers during the six-week impeachment trial. Realizing that he was near the end of his life, the Pennsylvania Abolitionist was determined to drive Johnson from office before taking his final breath.

President Johnson's defense team was bipartisan and included a cast of brilliant legal minds. The three Republicans included William Evarts (a prominent New York attorney and later Secretary of State), Benjamin R. Curtis (a Boston attorney and former Supreme Court Justice), and Henry Stanbery (who had resigned his position as Attorney General in order to defend Johnson). A.R. Nelson, a Union Loyalist and fellow Tennessean, also joined the defense team, along with Ohio Democrat, William S. Grouebeck.

Johnson maintained a low profile throughout the trial—a rare show of restraint by the fiery politician. Stanbery advised the President to refrain from giving newspaper interviews, warning him that it would "injure your case and embarrass your counsel." Privately, Johnson could barely contain his rage: "They have impeached me for a violation of the Constitution and laws. Have I not been struggling ever since I occupied this chair, to uphold the Constitution, which they are trampling under foot?"

On Saturday morning, March 7, 1868, the Sergeant-at-Arms of the Senate delivered a message, requesting President Johnson, or his representative, appear before the Senate to answer the impeachment charges. Johnson remained calm and uncharacteristically philosophical, as he discussed the summons with his private secretary, Colonel William Moore: "You know, Bill, I think many of those who have voted for impeachment feel more uneasy as to the position in which they have placed themselves, than I do as to the situation in which they have put me." The President's speculation about the ambivalence of many Republicans was accurate. Unlike their Radical colleagues, a number of Moderate Republican Senators were not hell bent to see Andrew Johnson's head on a political platter.

The impeachment trial was slated to begin on March 13th, but Henry Stanbery asked for a *40 day* postponement, so the President's defense team could mount a proper defense. Radical Republican Congressman (and House Manager), Benjamin Butler, erupted: "Forty days! As long as it took God to destroy the world by flood!" Ultimately, the defense was granted a *16 day* delay.

When an aide suggested that the President use the power of patronage to persuade Moderate Republicans to vote against conviction, Johnson bristled: "I will do nothing of the kind. If acquitted, I will not owe it to bribery. I would rather be convicted than buy my acquittal." Johnson's self-righteous avowal was disingenuous. Political patronage was indeed promised to certain lawmakers, in exchange for a *not guilty* vote. Evidence also suggests that nearly $100,000.00 was raised by Johnson supporters, and may have been used to bribe a small group of Senators to vote for acquittal.

Following the advice of his attorneys, Johnson did not attend the impeachment trial. Behind the scenes, however, the President remained vocal, criticizing the defense team, when he believed that their strategy was less than aggressive. On more than one occasion, a defiant Johnson threatened to deliver a speech on the floor of the Senate, proclaiming his innocence. In the end, Johnson somehow willed himself to stay away from Capitol Hill during the course of the trial.

The President's legal team launched a five-pronged defense: 1. The Tenure of Office Act was unconstitutional; 2. If the Tenure of Office Act was constitutional; it did not apply to Edwin Stanton, who had been appointed to office by Abraham Lincoln. The strictest interpretation of the law substantiated that premise—the Tenure of Office Act allowed the Chief Executive to legally dismiss appointed officials one month after the end of a single presidential term. Johnson's attorneys were quick to point out the Lincoln presidency ended in April of 1865 (at the time of his assassination), and the new President had waited nearly three years before firing the Secretary of War; 3. President Johnson was testing the constitutionality of the Tenure of Office Act, without criminal intent; 4. President Johnson had not technically violated the Act, because Stanton was still in office; 5. Impeachment was a *judicial* process and not a *political* one.

The defense maintained that any President could refuse to enforce a law that he deemed unconstitutional: "How can it be said that he had wrongful or unlawful intent, when the Constitution gave him the power to judge, for himself, in reference to the particular act?"

At 12:30 p.m. on March 30, 1868, Andrew Johnson's impeachment trial began under the watchful eye of Chief Justice Chase. The Senate gallery was crowded with eager onlookers, who were required to present a ticket for admission—only 1000 tickets were printed, and each Senator was allotted 4 passes to give family or constituents. For 6 weeks, Monday through Saturday, the Senate convened from noon until 5:00 p.m. Ironically, long-standing prejudices ruled the day, and blacks were not allowed to attend the impeachment proceedings.

In his opening statement for the prosecution, Representative Thaddeus Stevens announced the reason for the historic trial: "Mr. President (referring to the *President Pro Tempore* of the Senate), in obedience to the order of the House of Representatives and all the people of the United States, we do impeach Andrew Johnson,

President of the United States, of high crimes and misdemeanors in office."

For once in his life, Johnson refrained from taking his case to the people, denying opponents the opportunity to exploit his intemperate rhetoric. In private, however, he voiced considerable anger and disgust: "The American Senate is as corrupt as the Roman Senate!"

Massachusetts Senator, Charles Sumner, was convinced the President would be found guilty: "If Andrew Johnson is not guilty, then never was a political offender guilty before; and if his acquittal is taken as a precedent, never can a political offender be found guilty again. The proofs are mountainous."

On April 9, 1868, upon conclusion of the prosecution's case, former Supreme Court Justice, Ben Curtis, offered an opening statement for the defense. Closing arguments began thirteen days later.

During the early stages of the trial, most observers believed that Johnson would be convicted, and several newspapers speculated about the future of Senator Benjamin Wade. As *President Pro Tempore* of the Senate, the sixty-seven year-old Wade was next in line for the presidency, as there was no sitting Vice-President. The plain-spoken, sometimes profane Ohio Senator was known as the *Radical's Radical*, and had ardently supported harsh Reconstruction, black suffrage, and women's rights—a controversial issue in the mid-19th century.

While Wade's Radical Republican colleagues could hardly wait to dispose of Andrew Johnson, many Senators were none too happy about the prospect of the Ohioan ascending to the presidency. Many lawmakers felt it was improper for Wade to cast a vote in the impeachment trial, since a guilty verdict would propel into him into the White House, creating the ultimate conflict of interest. Some Moderate Republicans worried that Wade's liberal ideology, inflationary monetary policies, and support of high protective tariffs would alienate a large segment of the American electorate and jeopardize GOP victory in the upcoming presidential election.

Yet another political factor was at work. Chief Justice Chase disliked Benjamin Wade, believing his fellow Ohioan had cost him the 1860 presidential nomination. Eight years earlier, Wade's presidential candidacy had been a long shot, at best, while Chase had been a serious contender in the race against Abraham Lincoln. The Chief Justice still harbored presidential ambitions, and had quietly discussed the 1868 race with leaders of the rival Democratic Party, leading to speculation that Chase's personal animosity might influence his oversight of the impeachment trial.

Nonetheless, an overconfident Wade began openly discussing potential Cabinet appointments with General Grant, who was deemed the future of the Republican Party. The Senators holding Andrew Johnson's destiny in their hands were forced to decide if Benjamin Wade, as President, was the lesser of two evils. For six long weeks, the Moderate Republicans had ample opportunity to contemplate the immediate future of the presidency.

At the start of the trial, many of President Johnson's Cabinet officers were certain that he would be convicted, as were the majority of the nation's prominent newspapers. Gamblers wagered large sums on the outcome of the trial, leading some to fear that the betting might translate into outright bribery.

During the course of the impeachment trial, Edwin Stanton protected his own interests by refusing to leave the War Department. Fearful that Lorenzo Thomas might change the door locks, Stanton remained in his office, both day and night.

The 12th of May had been set as the date for the final vote, but when Radical Republican, Senator Jacob Howard took ill, Andrew Johnson's judgment day was postponed for four days. On May 15th, black churches throughout the Washington D.C. area offered joint prayers, imploring God to ordain a guilty verdict. At 12:30 p.m. on May 16, 1868, the Senate was called to order to render a verdict. The galleries were packed with news reporters and political observers, awaiting word of Johnson's fate.

By rule of law, the articles of impeachment were considered individually, with a 2/3rd majority necessary for conviction. The Radical Republicans proposed an immediate vote on article number 11, believing that the broad nature of those charges would likely result in a guilty verdict. Shortly after noon, Chief Justice Chase began the alphabetical roll call: "Mister Senator Anthony, how say you? Is the respondent, Andrew Johnson, President of the United States, guilty or not guilty of high misdemeanor, as charged in this article?"

"Guilty," Anthony replied.

Chase repeated the same question 53 times, until every Senator had recorded a voice vote. As the process unfolded, it became obvious the 2/3rd majority needed for conviction would come down to the votes of a handful of uncommitted Republicans. Excluding the unreconstructed members of the former Confederacy, there were 27 states represented in Congress, with a total of 54 Senators (42 Republicans and 12 Democrats). With *36* votes needed for conviction, the Republicans could only afford the loss of *6 guilty* ballots.

The suspense centered on Senator Edmund G. Ross of Kansas. Ross's predecessor, Jim Lane, a Conservative Republican, had supported Andrew Johnson by voting to uphold his veto of the Civil Rights Bill of 1866 and had introduced the bill recognizing the newly reconstructed state government of Arkansas. In response to Lane's support of Presidential Reconstruction, many Kansas Republicans were infuriated, and condemnation resolutions were introduced against him in the state legislature. Already in failing health and facing charges of financial improprieties, a humiliated Lane shot himself to death.

The Kansas state legislature elected Edmund Ross to fill Lane's vacant Senate seat. Ross was well known for his long-standing opposition to slavery, having been one of the Kansas legislators to introduce the condemnation resolution against Jim Lane. In 1854, the twenty-eight year-old Ross helped rescue a fugitive slave from a threatening mob, and shortly afterwards, changed his party affiliation from Democrat to Republican. He also joined Kansas' *Free State Army*, which battled pro-slavery forces in the state. In 1862, Ross enlisted in the Union Army, eventually rising to the rank of Major.

During his brief time in the Senate, Ross had voted in lock step with the Radical Republicans implementing Congressional Reconstruction. However, unlike most of his Republican colleagues, Ross refused to announce his impeachment vote in advance.

On May 16, 1868, the tension mounted as Chief Justice Chase proceeded with the roll call vote. A total of 24 out of the necessary 36 votes needed for conviction had been recorded when Chase reached the young Kansan's name: "Mister Senator Ross, how say you…?"

"Not guilty," Ross calmly replied.

The deciding ballot now rested in the hands of Peter G. Van Winkle of West Virginia, as the remaining Senators had already made it clear how they would vote.

"Mister Senator Van Winkle, how say you?" Chase asked, "Is the respondent, Andrew Johnson, guilty or not guilty of a high misdemeanor, as charged in this article?"

"Not guilty," Van Winkle announced.

It was over—*35* guilty votes and *19* not guilty votes—*1* shy of the 2/3rd majority needed for conviction. Andrew Johnson's presidency had been saved by the narrowest of margins. In the final analysis, all but 3 Democratic Senators voted not guilty, and were joined by *7* Republicans, who were labeled *Recusants*.

The Senate Republicans were stunned and voted to adjourn until May 26th, when the remaining articles of impeachment would be considered. During the ten-day recess, Edmund Ross was castigated and threatened by angry proponents of Johnson's impeachment. A telegram from his home state read: "Kansas repudiates you as she does all perjurers and skunks." A Kansas State Supreme Court Judge wired Ross: "The rope with which Judas Iscariot hanged himself is lost, but Jim Lane's pistol is at your service." An editorialist from the *New York Tribune* wrote that Ross was "a miserable poltroon and traitor."

On May 26th when the Senate reconvened, the 2nd and 3rd charges were put to a vote, and both fell *1* short of the necessary 2/3rd majority. Demoralized, the Radical Republicans realized their cause was lost, and voted for adjournment. The trial was officially concluded; Andrew Johnson had withstood an unprecedented constitutional crisis.

The seven Republican Recusants believed that their nonpartisan votes for acquittal were just and appropriate. Edmund Ross was certain that he had helped preserve the Constitution: "The impeachment of the President was an assault upon the principle of coordination that underlies our political system, and thus a menace to our established political forms, as, if successful, it would, logically, have been the practical destruction of the Executive Department." Badgered and verbally beaten, Ross confided to his wife: "Millions of men cursing me today will bless me tomorrow for having saved the country from the greatest peril through which it has ever passed, though none but God can ever know the struggle it cost me."

Angry and cynical, many Radical Republicans cried foul play, charging Senator Ross with trading his not guilty vote for the promise of presidential patronage. Whether or not it played a role in his impeachment vote, Ross was subsequently granted patronage over all presidential appointments in his home state of Kansas, as well as the territories of Colorado and New Mexico. In addition, Republican Senators Van Winkle, Fowler, and Grimes, all of whom voted for acquittal, had their requests for presidential appointments approved by Johnson.

The prospect of Benjamin Wade ascending to the presidency likely played a role in Johnson's acquittal. Three of the Recusants, Fessenden, Trumbull, and Grimes, simply did not like the President Pro Tempore.

Senator Lyman Trumbull of Illinois, defended his not guilty vote in practical terms, reminding his fellow Republican colleagues that Johnson's presidential term would expire in less than a year: "To convict and depose a Chief Magistrate of a great country, while his guilt was not made palpable by the record, and for insufficient cause, would be fraught with greater danger to the future of the country, than can arise from leaving Mr. Johnson in office for the remaining months of his term." Trumbull, who had drafted many of the Congressional Reconstruction legislative proposals vetoed by Johnson, received his share of harsh criticism. A fellow Illinois Republican warned him that "indignant people" in Chicago "would hang him to the most convenient lamppost."

The other Recusants, William Pitt Fessenden of Maine, John B. Henderson of Missouri, James W. Grimes of Iowa, Peter Van Winkle of West Virginia, and Joseph Smith Fowler of Tennessee, did not escape ostracism from peers, constituents, and the press. Henderson was burned in effigy in Missouri, while the *Wheeling Intelligencer* described Van Winkle as "West Virginia's betrayer." The Iowa press accused Grimes of "idiocy and impotency."

In the end, each of the Recusants defended their actions, but paid a heavy price. Joseph Fowler offered a courageous political epitaph: "I acted for my country and posterity in obedience to the will of God." All seven lost their Senate re-election bids.

Following Johnson's acquittal, Thaddeus Stevens was outraged: "The country is going to the Devil!" On July 7, 1868, a physically weak, yet determined Stevens introduced 5 new articles of impeachment against Johnson; on that same day, Stevens' Pennsylvania colleague, Thomas Williams, offered 14 charges of his own. Realizing that conviction was unlikely, the House of Representatives declined to pursue any further impeachment charges.

Thaddeus Stevens died five weeks later, without achieving his goal of driving Andrew Johnson from office. Later in life, Johnson revealed a measure of respect for his fierce opponent and frequent tormenter: "Old Thad Stevens was the most honest among them."

Another Radical, Representative Benjamin Butler, believed the motivation of the Recusants was less than honorable: "How does it happen that just enough and no more, Republican Senators, are convinced of the President's innocence? I think we shall be able to show where some of these men got their consciences, and how much they are worth."

For Benjamin Wade, who would have become President upon Johnson's conviction, further disappointment would follow. During the 1868 Republican National Convention, the radical Ohioan, whose policies were considered too liberal, was bypassed for the vice-presidential nomination.

After President Johnson was acquitted, the man at the center of the controversy, Edwin Stanton, resigned his position as Secretary of War. A year and half later, the new President, Ulysses S. Grant, nominated Stanton for a vacant seat on the United States Supreme

Court. Stanton died four days after taking the oath of office, and never took his place on the Supreme Court.

The outcome of Johnson's failed impeachment trial lent itself to different interpretations. While the Radical Republicans believed the process had been corrupt, President Johnson was certain that his acquittal validated the constitutional principle of separation of powers among the three branches of federal government. Historian, Lewis Gould, offered a succinct overview of Johnson's acquittal, describing the impeachment proceedings as "political, not criminal, and even on that score, the evidence was ambiguous."

Andrew Johnson did not live to see the vindication of his basic premise. In 1887, Congress repealed the Tenure of Office Act. In 1926, the U.S. Supreme Court ruled the law unconstitutional, after reviewing a case related to presidential dismissal of postmasters (*Myers v. U.S.*).

Johnson's wife, Eliza, offered the simplest explanation: "I knew he'd be acquitted. I knew it."

Chapter 18

His appearance is remarkable

As expected, at the Republican National Convention in late May of 1868, Ulysses S. Grant was unanimously nominated as the party's presidential candidate. Speaker of the House, Schuyler Colfax, was chosen as Grant's running mate. With the Civil War hero heading the ticket, the prospects of a Republican victory in November appeared strong.

While President Johnson had survived impeachment, the Republicans maintained solid majorities in both houses of Congress. Not surprisingly, lawmakers refused to readmit the former Confederate States into the Union until after the November election, to prevent Southern Democrats from influencing the presidential contest. Maintaining veto-proof majorities, congressional Republicans continued to dictate the policies and pace of Reconstruction.

The impeachment trial failed to diminish Johnson's ardor for States' Rights. On June 20, 1868, the President vetoed a bill readmitting Arkansas to the Union under a new state Constitution that mandated black suffrage and required voters to take an oath affirming their belief in racial equality. Less than a week later, Johnson vetoed an *omnibus* bill readmitting North Carolina, South Carolina, Florida, Georgia, Alabama, and Louisiana to the Union. Both vetoes were promptly overridden by Congress.

On July 4th, Johnson issued a *Proclamation of General Amnesty* for all Southerners who had participated in the rebellion, excluding those under indictment. Only a few ex-Confederates were not covered by the executive order, including Jefferson Davis, John C. Breckenridge (former CSA Secretary of War), and Robert E. Lee.

Johnson held onto slim hopes of receiving the Democratic presidential nomination. As an incumbent, Johnson should have been a formidable political foe for any challenger, but his popularity had steadily declined after the impeachment debacle. Johnson stated his case in a conversation with his secretary: "Why should they not take me up? They profess to accept my measures; they say I have stood by the Constitution and made a noble struggle. It is true, I am asked, why don't I join the Democratic Party. Why don't they join me?" Johnson vainly hoped to convince Democratic leaders that his name atop the presidential ticket was the best way to prevent the spread of racial equality across the South.

At best, Johnson was a controversial figure, and Democratic leaders considered him unelectable. Nonetheless, Johnson dispatched political operatives to New York City, when the Democratic National Convention opened on July 4, 1868. Johnson finished *second* on the first ballot, all of his votes coming from Southern and Border States. From that point forward, support for the incumbent President quickly evaporated. Horatio Seymour, the former Governor of New York, ultimately won the nomination. Demonized by the Republicans, Johnson had now been shunned by his own party.

After the convention, Andrew Johnson was the lamest of ducks. For the sake of party loyalty, Johnson actively supported Horatio Seymour and his running mate, Frank Blair of Missouri. On July 20th, Johnson vetoed a bill which excluded the unreconstructed states of Virginia, Mississippi, and Texas from the Electoral College, all three of which would have likely voted for Seymour. Yet again, Congress overrode his veto.

In many respects, the presidential election of 1868 was a symbolic reflection of the Civil War. The Democratic platform supported abolishment of the Freedmen's Bureau and establishment of "a government by white men, of white men, and for white men." The platform also denounced Military Reconstruction as unconstitutional, and called for state-controlled suffrage. The Democrats accused their Republican opponents of promoting "military despotism and Negro supremacy."

The Republican Party was eager to "wave the bloody shirt" of the Civil War and remind Northern voters that most Southerners remained *unrepentant*. The GOP advocated "equal suffrage to all loyal men" in the South, but hypocritically declared that all "loyal states" should be allowed to decide black suffrage on their own. Radical Republican Senator, Oliver Morton of Indiana, launched a scathing attack against the opposition party: "In short, the Democratic Party may be described as a common sewer and loathsome receptacle, into which I emptied every element of inhumanity and barbarism, which has dishonored the age."

Johnson and his fellow Democrats were disappointed when Ulysses S. Grant was swept into office in November of 1868. The 46-year-old Grant (the youngest man to have ever been elected President) won just under 53 percent of the popular votes, but decisively triumphed in the Electoral College (214 to 80). Nationwide, Horatio Seymour won the majority of white votes, but newly enfranchised freedmen put Grant over the top. The Republican ticket won 6 of the 7 Southern states that had been readmitted to the Union, where there were large pockets of eligible black voters. In February of 1869, recognizing the need for black votes in future elections, the Republican-controlled Congress passed the 15th Amendment, which constitutionally guaranteed black suffrage.

In the final months of his presidency, Andrew Johnson enjoyed few triumphs. Against his wishes, the 14th Amendment had been ratified by a requisite 3/4 majority of the states in July of 1868. Congress also overrode Johnson's veto of another bill extending the Freedmen's Bureau.

With vain hopes of limiting the power of the federal government, President Johnson proposed significant electoral reform, calling for election of the President to a single six-year term, popular election of the President (rather than use of the Electoral College), election of Supreme Court justices to twelve-year terms (rather than lifetime appointments), and direct popular election of United States

Senators (rather than election by state legislatures). As expected, the Republican controlled Congress summarily rejected Johnson's proposals.

The Johnson Administration, in spite of its many failures, did manage to achieve a measure of success. Spearheaded by Secretary of State William Seward, the United States purchased the Alaskan Territory from Russia. Many observers poked fun at the acquisition, derisively labeling it as *Seward's Folly*, *Seward's Icebox*, and *Johnson's Polar Bear Garden*. By a single vote, Congress reluctantly ratified the treaty. Later, when vast oil and gold deposits were discovered in Alaska, the purchase price of 2.5 cents per acre for the 7.2 million acres (twice the size of the state of Texas) proved a colossal bargain. Seward also paved the way for America's annexation of Midway Island.

The Secretary of State successfully negotiated a settlement with France, after the European power occupied portions of Mexico in 1861 and installed Archduke Maximilian of Austria as a puppet ruler, in obvious violation of the Monroe Doctrine. The United States responded by sending 50,000 troops to Mexico, shortly after the Civil War ended. Prodded by Seward, Napoleon III eventually withdrew his military forces, averting war with the United States.

The Johnson Administration mended fraying relations with Great Britain by enforcing neutrality laws against Irish American Fenians, who had been launching armed raids into Canada. Johnson also settled Civil War claims against England, related to British-built Confederate warships, which had sunk Union military and commercial shipping vessels.

Significant progress toward completion of the transcontinental railroad also occurred during the Johnson presidency. The transatlantic cable was completed in 1866, facilitating rapid communication between the United States and Europe.

Johnson also welcomed Queen Emma of the Sandwich Islands to the White House, marking the first such visit by royalty. The Pacific island ruler presented the President and First Lady with an ivory basket as a token of appreciation. Johnson also hosted a White House visit by British novelist, Charles Dickens.

In December of 1868, President Johnson delivered his final congressional address, lambasting Military Reconstruction: "The attempt to place the white population under the domination of persons of color in the South has impaired, if not destroyed, the friendly relations that had previously existed between them; and mutual distrust has engendered a feeling of animosity which, leading in some instances to collision and bloodshed, has prevented that cooperation between the two races, so essential to the successes of industrial enterprise in the Southern states." Johnson's admonition to Congress was rooted in his conviction concerning the justness of lenient Reconstruction. As Johnson predicted, harsh Congressional Reconstruction policies led to widespread racial polarization in the Deep South; an outcome the President believed he could have circumvented.

Unpopular throughout much of the country, Johnson managed to hold onto a few loyal supporters. Secretary of the Navy, Gideon Welles, was one of only a few prominent figures to defend Johnson, asserting that Presidential Reconstruction "had commenced with Mr. Lincoln, and I believed it correct."

For the remainder of his life, Johnson repeatedly criticized the Tenure of Office Act. He steadfastly maintained that the law, which wrecked his presidency, was unconstitutional; an opinion later validated by the Supreme Court. While Congress uncompromisingly implemented and enforced Reconstruction laws, President Johnson continued to demonstrate leniency. By the end of his presidency, Johnson had issued 13,914 pardons—13,350 of those were granted to supporters of the Confederacy.

On Christmas Day, 1868, President Johnson issued his fourth and final *Amnesty Proclamation*, pardoning, "unconditionally and without reservation," all persons who participated in the rebellion. At long last, even Jefferson Davis was included in this blanket amnesty. Johnson also pardoned the surviving conspirators in the assassination of Abraham Lincoln—Dr. Samuel Mudd, Edman Spangler, and Samuel Arnold. However, the President stubbornly refused to rescind the proclamation, dated May 4, 1865, implicating Jefferson Davis and other Confederate leaders in a *conspiracy* to assassinate President Lincoln. Johnson later confided that the biggest disappointment of his presidency was not seeing Davis hung for treason.

On December 30, 1868, Andrew Johnson celebrated his 60th birthday. In the final days of his Administration, Johnson remained active and upbeat, and seemingly possessed the vitality and mental energy of a younger man. A White House reporter closely observed the President: "His appearance is remarkable. The dark eyes are deep set, and peer out like shining orbs under a massive brow, on each side of which fall a lock of raven hair; below, the nose is aquiline and the mouth, firm set and vigorous, with an expression of determination bordering on obstinacy."

On February 26, 1869, contrary to the wishes of the lame duck President, Congress passed the 15th Amendment. The constitutional revision specified that "the right of citizens of the United States to vote shall not be denied or abridged by the United States or by any state on account of race, color, or previous condition of servitude. The amendment guaranteed universal male suffrage, with the exception of Indians. On March 3, 1870, during the Grant Administration, the amendment became law, after ratification by a 3/4 majority of the states.

The animosity between the outgoing and incoming Presidents deepened in the weeks following Grant's election. Johnson characterized his successor as a *disloyal* Radical, and predicted that Grant would be controlled and dominated by the Congress. With equal bluntness, Grant castigated his predecessor as vindictive, impulsive, and unprincipled.

When the President-Elect refused to allow his children to attend a birthday celebration for Johnson's five grandchildren at the White House, their mutual dislike intensified. Grant further angered Johnson by skipping the President's New Year's Day reception. To the very end, Johnson doubted his successor possessed the temperament or skill to be President. Like many military heroes who have ascended to the presidency, Grant appeared rather naïve: "I am not the representative of a political party."

On the eve of Grant's inauguration, Johnson angered many Unionists by allowing the family of John Wilkes Booth to claim the assassin's remains. Booth had previously been buried in an unmarked grave, but was subsequently interred in the family burial plot in Baltimore's Greenmount Cemetery.

On the morning of Inauguration Day, March 4, 1869, Johnson met with his Cabinet one last time. President-Elect Grant had made it clear that he would not ride to Capitol Hill in the same carriage with the outgoing President. In response to Grant's snub, Johnson refused to attend his successor's inaugural ceremony. Shortly after midday, as the echo of cannon fire signaled the beginning of the Grant presidency, Andrew Johnson quietly took leave from the White House.

Chapter 19

Thank God, for the vindication

For the first time in nearly thirty years, Andrew Johnson was in political exile. After remaining in Washington for two weeks to enjoy the hospitality of those friends and colleagues who had remained loyal during the tumultuous months of his presidency, Johnson boarded a train for home. Traveling across Virginia into Tennessee, the ex-President was surprised by the enthusiastic crowds cheering him along the way. In his hometown of Greeneville, a large *Welcome Home* banner was unfurled.

Johnson had invested his money wisely throughout his career, and managed to accumulate enough wealth to avoid the necessity of returning to work. Johnson's fortune was estimated to be in excess of $200,000.00, making him the wealthiest man in Greeneville. His 350-acre farm, just outside town, continued to generate profits from its twin flourmills.

At a time when the former President should have been able to reflect upon and enjoy the satisfaction of a remarkable life, the suicide of his son, Robert, in 1869, marred his retirement. Only thirty-five years old at the time of his death, Robert Johnson had been unable to escape the vicious cycle of alcoholism. Inside of ten years, Andrew and Eliza Johnson had endured the tragic deaths of two sons and a son-in-law.

In his retirement, Johnson suffered from painful bouts of kidney stones and continued discomfort from his injured elbowed. In 1873, he contracted life-threatening cholera. Convinced the end was near, Johnson prepared a final statement: "Here I will rest in quiet and peace, beyond the reach of Calumny's poisoned shaft, the influence of envy and jealous enemies…"

Johnson ultimately survived the cholera, and was well enough to travel to Washington D.C. for the graduation of his son, Frank, from Georgetown University. While visiting the nation's capitol, Johnson expressed his dissatisfaction with the Grant Administration. In an interview with a *New York Herald* reporter, the former President castigated his successor: "The little fellow has nothing in him. He hasn't a single idea. He has no policy—no conception of what the country requires…He is malicious, cunning, and treacherous." Johnson was delighted by the results of the 1870 mid-term elections when the Democrats gained 41 seats in the House of Representatives and 6 Senate seats.

The ever-ambitious former President was eager to recast his legacy. In April of 1869, he boasted of his accomplishments while serving as Military Governor of Tennessee: "I want my reputation to go down clear. There was not a colored man in Tennessee freed by Mr. Lincoln's Emancipation Proclamation. Who did it? I did, on the steps of the Capitol in Nashville, in the midst of the excitement and perils of that hour, while the missiles of death were flying. I, myself, proclaimed that slavery no longer existed in Tennessee; that every man was free by inherent principle in him."

Dissatisfied with the pace of life outside the political arena, Andrew Johnson longed to return to public office. In 1869, he lost a close race for the United States Senate, when the Tennessee state legislature elected Johnson's opponent by the narrow margin of 55 to 51; this was his first electoral loss since 1837. Johnson's desire to seek elective office, however, was not diminished by defeat. In a letter to his son, Frank, he complained of life in Greeneville: "It is a dull place, and likely to continue so." He further described the small town as "lifeless as a graveyard."

When Ulysses S. Grant decided to run for a second term as President, Johnson actively campaigned on behalf of the Democratic candidate, Horace Greeley. Johnson attacked Grant at every opportunity, accusing the incumbent President of accepting bribes and "running up" the national debt. Johnson's negative campaigning proved to be of little consequence, when Grant was re-elected with 53 percent of the popular vote, and an overwhelming electoral majority of 214 to 80.

In 1872, Johnson once again sought public office, running for an *at large* congressional seat, but finished third in the voting. Two years later, he once again declared his candidacy for the United States Senate, and promised to take his case to the people: "The agricultural and industrial classes constitute, by far, the most numerous and influential of all the classes. They combine, too, more of the elements of integrity. They are more truthful and reliable. Their very occupations lead them in the paths of favor and honorable dealing."

As he traveled around the state, Johnson lobbied for one final chance to represent Tennessee at the national level: "If I could be returned to the U.S. Senate, in accordance with popular sentiment reflected by the legislature, it would be appreciated by me as the greatest compliment of my life, and be a deserved rebuke to treachery and ingratitude."

Populism and persistence finally paid off for Johnson. On January 26, 1875, on the 54th ballot, by a 1 vote margin, the Tennessee state legislature elected him to the United States Senate. Learning of his hard fought victory, Johnson was elated: "Well, well, well, I'd rather have this information than to learn I had been elected President of the United States. Thank God, for the vindication!"

Chapter 20

Able and timely

When Andrew Johnson returned to the United States Senate in 1875, it marked the first and only time in American history that a former President has served in that legislative body. Johnson's return to Capitol Hill drew nationwide interest, including an article in the *Cincinnati Commercial*: "With Andrew Johnson in the Senate, we can dismiss all fears for the safety of the Constitution."

In March of 1875, Johnson joined the 44th Congress. As Reconstruction neared its conclusion, the balance of power on Capitol Hill was gradually shifting. The Democrats had won control of the House of Representatives for the first time since the end of the Civil War, and had narrowed the Republican majority in the Senate.

Johnson established residence at the Imperial Hotel, as he began his second stint in the Senate. On March 5th, he was sworn into office by Vice-President Henry Wilson, who, only seven years earlier, had voted *guilty* in Johnson's impeachment trial. At first, the controversial former President was uncertain about how he would be received. Those doubts were laid to rest, when Johnson found a floral bouquet on his desk in the Senate chambers. As he prepared to take his seat, Johnson's Senate colleagues and members of the gallery burst into applause. For the first time since his departure from Washington under the cloud of impeachment, The Loyalist was able to appreciate a measure of redemption.

Many of Andrew Johnson's harshest critics reassessed the Tennessean's role in history. The *New York Times*, which had repeatedly attacked Johnson during his presidency, described him as "a man of great natural abilities and force of character."

On March 20, 1875, Johnson took the floor of the Senate to deliver his only public address. He criticized the Grant Administration for using military force to interfere with elections in Louisiana, declaring that such policies were indicative of the current President's desire to establish a White House dynasty. Johnson predicted Grant's election to a third term would result in a "farewell to the liberties of the country."

Nashville's *Union and American*, characterized Johnson's Senate speech as "able and timely," and "a stirring appeal to save the country and the Constitution." The former President was delighted to have lived long enough to witness public acknowledgment of his long-standing defense of constitutional principles, and took particular satisfaction in the partial exoneration of his good name.

After Congress recessed in the spring of 1875, Andrew Johnson returned to Greeneville for a brief visit. Ever restless, he scheduled a trip to Ohio to campaign for Democratic candidates in the upcoming election.

On July 28th, Johnson left Greeneville by train, encountering two old friends, who were fellow passengers. In the course of ensuing conversations, Johnson reflected on the problems that plagued his presidency, blaming Edwin Stanton for many of his difficulties. He described the former Secretary of War as "the Marat of American politics"—alluding to Jean-Paul Marat, the radical physician, journalist, and politician, made famous by the French Revolution. Johnson further characterized Stanton as a "very bitter, uncompromising, and self-assertive man." Now on a roll, he regurgitated an unsubstantiated rumor, blaming Stanton for the assassination of Abraham Lincoln. According to Johnson, the Secretary of War had convinced Lincoln to not commute the death sentence of one of John Wilkes Booth's friends, which led the actor to seek vengeance against the President. He also alleged that Mary Suratt had been innocent, accusing Stanton of withholding evidence from Booth's diary, thereby railroading her into execution.

As the conversation progressed, Johnson defended Presidential Reconstruction. He reminded his travel companions that he had endeavored to preserve the Constitution, and "protect the South against unreasonable hatred." In Johnson's opinion, the murder of Abraham Lincoln had incited Congress to employ unconstitutional powers.

When the train reached Carter Station, Tennessee, Johnson disembarked and took a carriage to his daughter's house in nearby Elizabethton; the stopping point for this leg of his journey. After dinner that evening, Johnson conversed with his granddaughter, Lillie. While chatting with her grandfather, Lillie was momentarily distracted by activities in the yard, and looked out the window. Suddenly, there was a loud crash, as Johnson fell from his armchair onto the floor.

Having suffered a major stroke, Johnson's left side was paralyzed and his speech was slurred. After being helped into bed, the former President assured his family that he would soon feel better, and instructed them to refrain from calling a doctor. However, when Johnson's condition failed to improve, two physicians from Elizabethton were summoned. For a brief period, the former President rallied, and was able to engage in rational conversations with the doctors and his family members, but the improvement proved short lived. On Friday night, July 30th, the patient suffered a second stroke, and lost consciousness. At half-past two the following morning, Johnson, who was sixty-six years old, died.

On August 3, 1875, Andrew Johnson was buried on Greeneville's *Signal Hill*, which was so named for its elevation and commanding view of the surrounding landscape. Johnson had purchased the property in 1852, and often visited his future gravesite to enjoy the panoramic view of the nearby Great Smoky Mountains.

As he had requested, the ex-President's body was wrapped in an American flag, with his head placed atop his personal copy of the United States Constitution. Johnson's casket lay in state in the parlor of his home, as well as in the county courthouse. The entire town of Greeneville was draped in black, while church bells tolled in mourning. On the day of his burial, some 5,000 people accompanied the casket to Signal Hill, where Johnson received the burial rites afforded to long-standing Masons—an organization he had joined in his early adulthood.

In Washington D.C., government business was halted on the day of Johnson's funeral. Federal office buildings, like the homes and businesses in Johnson's hometown, were draped in black. President Grant, Johnson's arch enemy, offered a gracious tribute, describing the former President as the "last survivor of his honored predecessors."

Across the South, The Loyalist, once vilified as a traitor to his region, was hailed for his efforts to implement a fair Reconstruction plan. The *Arkansas Gazette* mourned Johnson's passing: "But for him, after the war, our beloved South would have been ruined beyond redemption."

Johnson's wife, Eliza, died less than six months after her husband, and was buried beside him on Signal Hill. In 1878, local citizens erected a monument at Johnson's grave. Topped by an eagle, the obelisk bears the image of a hand atop an opened Bible. The inscription on the marker would likely have pleased Johnson: *CONSTITUTION OF THE UNITED STATES.*

The Johnson gravesite eventually became known as *Monument Hill*, and remained in family hands, until 1906, when it was designated as the *Andrew Johnson National Cemetery.* The War Department maintained the area until 1942, when it was transferred to the National Park Service. Johnson's children (the bodies of Robert and Charles were exhumed and interred on Monument Hill), grandchildren, and other descendents were later buried at the historic site.

The marble stone marking the grave of the 17th President of United States defines his legacy:

Andrew Johnson
Born December 29, 1808
Died July 31, 1875
HIS FAITH IN THE PEOPLE NEVER WAIVERED

EPILOGUE

If Abraham Lincoln had not been assassinated at the height of his popularity, would Reconstruction have followed a different course? Absent Lincoln's murder, would the name Andrew Johnson be remembered anywhere outside the state of Tennessee? A century and half after the Civil War, there is no clear answer to those questions. Historians occupy themselves with chronicling *what did* happen, while contemplating *what might have* happened. Abraham Lincoln, himself, once remarked: "The best thing about the future is that it comes only one day at a time."

The Great Emancipator's unfulfilled plans for Reconstruction will never be completely known. Lincoln's Ten Percent Plan and pocket veto of the Wade-Davis Bill suggest that he intended to pursue a *lenient* Reconstruction. Blessed with wisdom, patience, and political adroitness, Lincoln would most assuredly have handled the confrontation with congressional Radical Republicans in a less acrimonious manner than his successor. In sharp contrast to Johnson's unbending mind set, Lincoln possessed the ability to reassess situations and change his course of action, when necessary. It is almost inconceivable to contemplate the House of Representatives attempting to impeach Abraham Lincoln.

In sharp contrast to Lincoln, Andrew Johnson was stubborn and hypersensitive; once his mind was set, he seldom changed positions. Johnson's interpretation of the Constitution advocated States' Rights, to the exclusion of secession, with minimal intervention by the federal government. Johnson was also a racist, hardly an anomaly for most white Americans of his generation, and his prejudice blinded him to the wrongful discriminatory practices of the former Confederate States.

Unlike Lincoln, Andrew Johnson was no match for the Radical Republicans. Once Republican lawmakers achieved veto-proof majorities, Presidential Reconstruction was doomed, and Congressional Reconstruction became the law of the land in the former Confederacy. Military governments, dominated by former Northerners (*Carpetbaggers*), Southern Union Loyalists (*Scalawags*), and *freed slaves*, took control of state governments and occupied a handful of previously, all-white congressional seats, as well as numerous state and local offices.

On March 30, 1870, the 15th Amendment was ratified, prohibiting denial of voting rights based on race or previous servitude. Excluding Tennessee, which had been readmitted to the Union prior to the onset of Congressional Reconstruction, the ten other Confederate States were governed by martial law.

Beginning with Arkansas, on June 22, 1868, and concluding with Georgia, on July 15, 1870, the remaining Southern states were eventually readmitted to the Union. The *reunification*, however, was punctuated with discord. Throughout the Deep South, white Conservatives chafed under military rule, and resented the election of black men to positions of leadership, spawning the formation of secret societies promoting white supremacy—most notably the *Ku Klux Klan*.

The Ku Klux Klan was founded in Pulaski, Tennessee in 1866, with ex-Confederate General, Nathan Bedford Forrest, serving as the first *Grand Wizard*. Between 1868 and 1871, nearly 4,000 blacks were lynched by the Klan and other vigilante groups.

During the Grant Administration, after the passage of the *Ku Klux Klan Act*, the Justice Department targeted white supremacists. Some 600 Klansmen were convicted of racially motivated crimes against freedmen, and the KKK's influence eventually waned during the latter portion of the 19th century.

In 1869, Mississippi's Hiram Revels became the first African American to be elected to the United States Senate. Ironically, another black Mississippian, Blanche K. Bruce, was elected to fill the Senate seat once occupied by Jefferson Davis.

Large numbers of freed blacks were elected to local and state offices, but few made it to Congress. Because of the apportionment of voting districts, white majorities were able to control the outcome of most congressional races. Between 1870 and 1876, *fif-teen* African Americans, all Republicans, were elected to the House of Representatives (along with *two* Senators). Among those Congressmen, *six* came from South Carolina, where the black population was proportionally higher and more evenly distributed than other Southern states. Most of the black lawmakers served only one or two terms.

In Louisiana, a freedman was elected Governor. African Americans were also elected Lieutenant Governor in *six* states, and Secretary of State in *seven* more.

In May of 1874, Speaker of the House James Blaine handed his gavel to Congressman Joseph Rainey of South Carolina. Rainey, who had worked as a barber on a Confederate blockade-runner during the Civil War, became the first black man to preside over the United States House of Representatives.

While the newly elected, racially mixed, state and local governments were progressive, as exemplified by the establishment of publicly funded state education facilities, waste and corruption also abounded. The governmental scandals reinforced the prejudices of white Southerners, who had long-maintained that blacks were incapable of self-rule. Andrew Johnson was certain that his prophetic warnings had come to fruition—Congressional Reconstruction had generated "a feeling of opposition and hatred between the two races, which, becoming deep-rooted and ineradicable would prevent them from living together in a state of mutual friendliness."

Andrew Johnson's concerns about the leadership skills of his presidential successor proved prescient. The Radical Republicans in Congress viewed Ulysses S. Grant as a pawn, and grew accustomed to dictating policy to the President. Grant's personal and professional associations ultimately brought considerable embarrassment to the presidency, as his private secretary (Orville E. Babcock), Secretary of War (William W. Belknap), and at least one family member were implicated in financial scandals. At the conclusion of his second term, Grant's own words betrayed Johnson's prophesy: "It was my fortune, or misfortune, to be called to the office of Chief Executive, without any previous political training."

Congressional Reconstruction lasted for a decade, and ended after a political compromise following the 1876 presidential election. Hoping to extend their White House reign, the Republican Party selected another Civil War hero, Ohio Governor, Rutherford B. Hayes, as its nominee. The forty-six year-old Hayes had risen to the rank of Brigadier General in the Union Army, and was decorated for valor, after being wounded four times and having four horses shot out from under him. While serving as an Ohio Congressman, Hayes followed in lock step with Radical Republican lawmakers, helping override President Johnson's vetoes of the Reconstruction Acts, and also voting for his impeachment.

On Election Day, Hayes' Democratic opponent, Governor Samuel Tilden of New York, outpolled the Republican candidate by nearly 250,000 popular votes. Tilden won 16 states and accumulated 184 electoral votes, 1 short of a majority, while Hayes carried 18 states and earned 165 electoral votes. Republican leaders immediately contested the election, alleging that black voters were prevented from voting in South Carolina, Louisiana, and Florida. The GOP also challenged returns from the state of Oregon. The allegations were not without merit, as Florida, Louisiana, and South Carolina, all of which had dense pockets of Republican voters, submitted 2 sets of electoral returns with opposite outcomes—both vote counts were legally certified by different official registrars. With the election in doubt, the country waited for 3 months to learn of the true victor. Congress appointed a special commission, consisting of 5 Congressman, 5 Senators, and 5 Supreme Court Justices (8 Republicans and 7 Democrats), to decide the outcome of the presidential race.

On February 7, 1877, the commissioners awarded all 20 of the disputed electoral votes to Hayes in an 8 to 7, party line vote, giving the Republican candidate a razor-thin 185 to 184 electoral majority. In exchange for the favorable ruling, Hayes had agreed to withdraw all federal troops from the former Confederate states and appoint a Southerner to his Cabinet. The aptly named *Compromise of 1877* effectively ended Reconstruction. On April 24th of that same year, President Hayes ordered the final withdrawal of federal troops, bringing an end to military occupation of the former Confederacy. Hayes also appointed David Key of Tennessee as Postmaster General. Many joyous Southerners christened the compromise as the *Redemption*.

Though Reconstruction was officially over, regional pride often trumped reconciliation. In 1881, Jefferson Davis published his two-volume memoirs, *The Rise and Fall of the Confederate Government*, which was welcomed by eager Southern readers. Above the Mason-Dixon Line, Davis' tome was greeted less enthusiastically.

When Davis died on December 6, 1889, his body was interred in a mausoleum at Metairie Cemetery in New Orleans. In Washington D.C., Secretary of War, Redfield Proctor, refused to lower departmental flags to half mast, even though Davis had once held the same office, during the administration of President Franklin Pierce.

Southerners found ways to sustain their memories of the heroic *War against Northern Aggression*. On May 28, 1893, Jefferson Davis' coffin was removed from its crypt in New Orleans and placed aboard a train bound for Virginia. Over the course of 4 days, the train snaked its way across Mississippi, Alabama, Georgia, South Carolina, North Carolina, and Virginia, with several stops along the way, allowing Southerners to pay respects to their beloved, former Commander-in-Chief. On May 31st, Davis was reinterred at Richmond's Hollywood Cemetery. On June 3, 1907, the 99th anniversary of Davis' birth, a bronze monument was dedicated in his honor in the former Confederate capitol. Those in attendance at the dedication ceremony continued to believe that the *South would rise again*.

When Reconstruction ended, white Democrats quickly seized control of local and state governments in the Deep South. State legislatures enacted new laws and rewrote their Constitutions, effectively ending the so-called *Nigger Rule*. With the return of *Home Rule*, the loathsome era of *Jim Crow* became an ugly way of life in the South.

Poll taxes, selective and discriminatory literacy tests, and outright intimidation by white vigilantes effectively disenfranchised the vast majority of Southern blacks. Blatant discrimination became a way of life, with clearly demarcated *white only* sections in the transportation, lodging, and food service industries.

Buttressed by bitter memories of Congressional Reconstruction, future generations exploited the States' Rights argument to perpetuate racial segregation. Politicians, like George C. Wallace, Strom Thurmond, and Jesse Helms, employed racially-coded populism as a springboard to electoral success.

Not until nearly 100 years after the Civil War did the federal government act in a meaningful fashion to end segregation and enforce non-discriminatory voting rights. Ironically, another Southerner with the last name of Johnson, who was thrust into office after the assassination of his predecessor, used the bully pulpit of the presidency to strong arm passage of civil rights legislation. The *Civil Rights Act of 1964* and the *Voting Rights Act of 1965* forced Southern states to end race based discrimination, and were the most significant accomplishments of Lyndon B. Johnson's presidency. The twin evils of slavery and racism, however, remain permanent stains in the fabric of American history.

Andrew Johnson's legacy is unique in many ways. His rise from self-educated, impoverished mudsill to President of the United States represents one of the greatest success stories in American history. As the only Southern lawmaker who refused to join the Secessionist movement, Johnson became the country's most renowned Loyalist.

As President, Andrew Johnson endured unprecedented repudiation by Congress—15 of his 20 vetoes were overridden, compared to only 4 out of 93 for his successor, Ulysses S. Grant. To date, only 2 Presidents have been impeached, but Johnson's single-vote acquittal was much narrower than President Bill Clinton's exoneration. Post-presidency, Johnson became the first and only former Chief Executive to win election to the United States Senate.

Can Andrew Johnson ever be fully understood? By nature, he was a loner and rarely confided his innermost feelings. While serving in public office, Johnson often lived apart from his loved ones, and only sparingly filled the void with long-lasting relationships outside of family.

An examination of Johnson's official papers reveal far more documents sent *to* him than those sent *from* him. Most of his correspondence was written by aides, and few documents are in Johnson's own hand—largely a by-product of his self-consciousness about poor grammar and erroneous spelling. Johnson never kept a diary, where many statesmen have traditionally recorded their private thoughts and feelings. Secretary of Navy, Gideon Welles, succinctly described Johnson as a man who "had no confidants and sought none."

In October of 2000, a group of 132 professors of history, law, and political science were asked by the *Federalist Society* and the *Wall Street Journal* to rate past Presidents on a scale of 1 to 5; 5 was highly superior and 1 was well below average. The survey was conducted during the Clinton presidency, thus excluding his successors, George W. Bush and Barak Obama. William Henry Harrison and James Garfield were also excluded from the rating, given the brief durations of their terms—both died shortly after their inaugurations. Andrew Johnson earned a score of 1.65, placing him number 36 on the list of 39. Only Franklin Pierce, James Buchanan, and Warren G. Harding received lower ratings.

As evidenced by this study, Andrew Johnson's presidency is viewed largely in a negative light. The failure of Presidential Reconstruction, his subsequent impeachment, and repudiation by his own party in the 1868 election irrevocably damaged Johnson's legacy. Johnson's contemporaries were often at odds in their assessment of his character. When he chose to remain in Congress after the outbreak of the Civil War, Jefferson Davis described Johnson as a "Southern Traitor," while the *New York Times* praised him as "the greatest man of his age."

Many who have written about Andrew Johnson have found it difficult to offer neutral opinions. A handful of historians and biographers admire his courage and devotion to constitutional principles, but a larger number condemn his intemperate personality and overt racism. Much of the condemnation is justified, and Johnson's vindictiveness most certainly contributed to his tarnished legacy. Impulsive, thin-skinned, and sometimes blatantly self-righteous, Johnson, often times, was his own worst enemy. He found it nearly impossible to separate political dissent from personal animosity. A long time bodyguard described Johnson as "the best hater I ever knew."

Johnson's overt racism obscured his lifelong, vigorous opposition to prejudice against the poor, white immigrants, and Catholics. Blinded by bigotry, Johnson was unable to fathom a society where blacks and whites enjoyed equal rights. Believing that his interpretation of the Constitution was infallible, Johnson stubbornly refused to collaborate with Conservative and Moderate Republican lawmakers to achieve a less acrimonious post-Civil War Reconstruction.

Perhaps Johnson biographer, Hans Trefousse, described Johnson most clearly: "A child of his time, but he failed to grow up with it." Historian, David O. Stewart, who has written extensively about Johnson's impeachment trial, offered a blunter assessment: "As President, Johnson inflicted more wounds on the nation than he healed." Stewart goes on to write: "Far from being Lincoln's political heir, Johnson squandered Lincoln's legacy."

Nonetheless, Andrew Johnson was a bold leader, who stood on principle. With fearlessness bordering on recklessness, *The Loyalist* never abandoned established positions, even during the most trying of times. Johnson biographer, Albert Castel, offers a fitting description of the former mudsill's burning ambition: "By nature, he was a seeker and user of power, who relied not on collaboration, but on determination to achieve his objectives."

Abraham Lincoln, who was no stranger to controversy, recognized Johnson's courage. After appointing him as the Military Governor of Tennessee, Lincoln offered a tribute that is as appropriate today, as it was a century and a half ago: "No man has a right to judge Andrew Johnson in any respect, who has not suffered so much as he for the nation's sake."

TIME LINE OF ANDREW JOHNSON'S LIFE

1808 Born on December 29th in Raleigh, North Carolina

1811 Johnson's father, Jacob, dies and leaves family further impoverished

1818 Enters into tailor's apprenticeship contract

1824 Flees North Carolina after committing an act of vandalism

1826 Along with his mother, stepfather, and brother, moves to Greeneville, Tennessee

1827 Opens tailor's shop in March, and marries Eliza McCredie on May, 17; Eliza ultimately gives birth to 5 children—Martha, Mary, Charles, Robert, and Andrew, Jr. (commonly referred to as Frank)

1829 Elected as Alderman in Greeneville

1830 Elected Mayor of Greeneville

1835 Elected to Tennessee state legislature

1837 Defeated in his re-election bid to the state legislature

1839 Re-elected to the state legislature

1840 Serves as Democratic presidential elector

1841 Elected to the Tennessee state senate

1843 Elected to U.S. House of Representatives (he was re-elected 4 times)

1853 Elected Governor of Tennessee

1855 Re-elected Governor of Tennessee

1857 Elected to U.S. Senate

1860 Declares himself a Loyalist and refuses to resign his seat in the U.S. Senate and join Secessionists

1862 Appointed Military Governor of Tennessee by President Lincoln

1864 Elected Vice-President of the United States on the National Union ticket

1865 Becomes President of the United States after the death of Abraham Lincoln on April 15th

1868 Impeached by the U.S. House of Representatives and avoids Senate conviction by a single vote

1869 Defeated in his bid for the U.S. Senate

1872 Defeated in his bid for U.S. House of Representatives

1874 Elected to the U.S. Senate—the only time in history that a former President is elected to that legislative body

1875 Dies on July 31st in Elizabethon, Tennessee at the age of 66

BIBLIOGRAPHY

Books:

Barber, James David. *The Presidential Character: Predictions of Performance in the White House.* Prentice-Hall, 1985.

Benedict, Michael Les. *The Impeachment Trial of Andrew Johnson.* W.W. Norton & Company, 1973.

Bennett, William J. and John T. E. Cribb. *The Patriot's Almanac.* Thomas Nelson, 2008.

Bowen, David Warren. *Andrew Johnson and the Negro.* University of Tennessee Press, 1989.

Brooks, Stewart M. *Our Assassinated Presidents: The True Medical Stories.* Bell Publishing Company, 1956.

Campbell, Tracy. Deliver the Vote: *A History of Election Fraud, and American Political Tradition, 1792-2004.* Carroll & Graff, 2005.

Carwardine, Richard. Lincoln: *A Life of Purpose and Power.* Alfred A. Knopf, 2003.

Castel, Albert. *The Presidency of Andrew Johnson.* University Press of Kansas, 1979.

Countryman, Edward. Americans: *A Collision of Histories.* Hill & Wang, 1996.

Crane, William D. *Andrew Johnson*: *Tailor from Tennessee*. Dodd, Mead & Company, 1968.

Dallek, Robert. *Hail to the Chief*: *The Making and Unmaking of American Presidents*. Hyperion, 1996.

Donald, David Herbert. *Lincoln*. Simon & Schuster, 1995.

Douglas, Frederick. *The Life and Times of Frederick Douglas from 1817 to 1882 as Written by Himself.* 1882.

Du Bois, W. E. B. *Black Reconstruction in America, 1860-1880*. Antheneum: 1992.

Foote, Shelby. *The Civil War, a Narrative*: *Fort Sumter to Perryville*. Random House, 1958.

Foote, Shelby. *The Civil War, a Narrative*: *Fredericksburg to Meridian*. Random House, 1963.

Foote, Shelby. *The Civil War, a Narrative*: *Red River to Appomattox*. Random House, 1974.

Goodwin, Doris Kearns. *Team of Rivals*: *The Political Genius of Abraham Lincoln*. Simon & Schuster, 2005.

Gordon-Reed, Annette. *Andrew Johnson*. Times Books, 2011.

Gould, Lewis. *Grand Old Party: A History of the Republicans.* Random House, 2003.

Johnson, Andrew. *President U.S., 1808-1875*: *Papers, 1814-1900*. University of Maryland: McKeldin Library, 2006.

Kaltman, Al. *Cigars, Whiskey, and Winning: Leadership Lessons from General Ulysses S. Grant.* Prentice Hall Press, 1998.

Kennedy, John F. *Profiles in Courage.* Harper & Brothers, 1956.

Kunhardt III, Philip B. and Peter W. Kunhardt and Peter W. Kunhardt, Jr. *Looking for Lincoln.* Alfred A. Knopf, 2008.

Maslowski, Peter. *Treason Must Be Made Odious: Military Occupation and Wartime Reconstruction in Nashville, Tennessee, 1862-1865.* KTO Press, 1978.

McKitrick, Eric L. *Andrew Johnson and Reconstruction.* Oxford University Press, 1960.

McPherson, James. *The Battle Cry of Freedom.* Oxford University Press, 1988.

Means, Howard. *The Avenger Takes His Place: Andrew Johnson and the 45 Days that Changed the Nation.* Harcourt, Inc., 2006.

Oreilly, Bill and Martin Dugard. *Killing Lincoln: The Shocking Assassination that Changed America Forever.* Henry Holt and Company, 2011.

Paludan, Phillip Shaw. *The Presidency of Abraham Lincoln.* University of Kansas Press, 1994.

Remini, Robert V. *The House: The History of the House of Representatives.* Smithsonian Books, 2006.

Steers Jr., Edward. *Blood on the Moon: The Assassination of Abraham Lincoln.* University of Kentucky Press, 2001.

Stewart, David O. *Impeached: The Trial of President Andrew Johnson and the Fight for Lincoln's Legacy.* Simon & Schuster, 2009.

Swanson, James L. *Manhunt: The 12 Day Chase for Lincoln's Killer.* Harper Collins Publishers, 2006.

Swanson, James L. *Blood Crimes: The Chase for Jefferson Davis and the Death Pageant for Lincoln's Corpse*. William Morrow, 2010.

Taranto, James and Leo, Leonard, Ed. *Presidential Leadership: Rating the Best and the Worst in the White House*. Free Press, 2004.

Trefousse, Hans. *Andrew Johnson: A Biography*. American Political Biography Press, 1998.

Trefousse, Hans. *Impeachment of a President: Andrew Johnson, the Blacks, and Reconstruction*. Fordham University Press, 1999.

Wallace, Chris. *Character: Profiles in Presidential Courage*. Rugged Land, 2004.

Whitcomb, John and Claire. *Real Life at the White House: 200 Years of Daily Life at America's Most Famous Residence*. Routledge, 2000.

Whitney, David. *The American Presidents, Eleventh Edition*. Direct Brands, 2009.

Website Sources:

www.law.umkc.edu
www.sonofthesouth.net
www.footnote.com
www.eyewitnesstohistory.com
www.findagrave.com
www.samuelmudd.com
www.globalsecurity.com
www.bioguide.congress.gov
www.iath.virginia.edu
www.ourdocuments.gov
www.nps.gov
www.pbs.org
www.mrlincolnandfreedom.org

www.bartleby.com
www.hitoricaltextarchive.edu
www.millercenter.virginia.edu
www.senate.gov
www.archive.org
www.tulane.edu
www.gutenberg.org
www.uselectionatlas.org
www.historymatters.gmu.edu
www.ajmuseum.tusculum.edu
www.discovergreeneville.com
www.whitehouse.gov
www.andrewjohnson.com
www.tngenweb.org
www.americancivilwarhistory.org
www.presidency.uscb.edu

On Site Resources:

President Andrew Johnson Museum and Library, Tusculum College, Greeneville, Tennessee

The Andrew Johnson National Historic Site, Greeneville, Tennessee

ACKOWLEDGEMENTS

This book is neither a comprehensive biography of the 17th President of the United States, nor a thorough study of the Civil War and Reconstruction. In concise fashion, I have endeavored to tell the story of an often misunderstood and controversial figure in American history, and the tumultuous events that shaped his life. I am indebted to those historians, living and dead, who are listed in the bibliography; the fruits of their labors have provided a valuable historical record.

I owe much to my wife, Anne, who indulges my passion for the writing project at hand. She has learned more about Andrew Johnson than she undoubtedly ever wanted to know. I love you very much. My sons, Andy and Ben, remain the lights of my life. I love you more than I can put into words.

Once again, Jim Fulmer gave graciously of his time to edit this work. This is our sixth book together, and, each time, he rises to the occasion. I am blessed to call you my friend.

I sincerely hope you found *The Loyalist: The Life and Times of Andrew Johnson* entertaining, informative, and thought provoking. Thank you for taking time to read this book.

ABOUT THE AUTHOR

Jeffrey Smith is a physician and writer. A native of Enterprise, Alabama, Dr. Smith received his undergraduate and medical degrees from the University of Alabama, and completed his residency at the William S. Hall Psychiatric Institute. Since 1990, he has worked in private practice in upstate South Carolina. Dr. Smith lives in Greer, South Carolina with his wife, Anne. They are the proud parents of two sons, Andy and Ben.

OTHER BOOKS BY JEFFREY K. SMITH

FICTION:

Sudden Despair

Two Down, Two to Go

A Phantom Killer

NON-FICTION:

Rendezvous in Dallas: The Assassination of John F. Kennedy

The Fighting Little Judge: The Life and Times of George C. Wallace

Fire in the Sky: The Story of the Atomic Bomb

Bad Blood: Lyndon B. Johnson, Robert F. Kennedy, and the Tumultuous 1960s

Dixiecrat: The Life and Times of Strom Thurmond

To learn more about these books, and purchase copies, please visit the author's website, www.newfrontierpublications.net.

30784967R00109

Made in the USA
Charleston, SC
24 June 2014